Fingerstyle Guitar Tunes

EARLY MUSIC GEMS

Raymond Gonzalez

Online Audio

To access the online audio recording go to:
WWW.MELBAY.COM/30919MEB

The ECO Pursuit Exotic S Concert CE White Sand guitar image is courtesy of Breedlove Guitar Company.

WWW.MELBAY.COM

Preface

Even after playing classical guitar professionally for decades, I found that many of the tunes in this collection were as new to me as I'm sure they will be to you. To the best of my ability, I have stayed true to the melodies of both vocal and instrumental compositions.

Unlike the previous volumes in this series, I kept to a more traditional rhythmic and harmonic language. Very occasionally you will find an unexpected moving voice or chordal resolution. I did my best to make use of traditional modes from the period. If these modes weren't immediately apparent in the music, I would then draw on my years of playing and study to incorporate modal harmonies which might sound unexpected to the modern Western ear but would be standard practice in the Renaissance and Middle Ages. In addition, as a lover of polyphony, I would make use of multi-layered voices whenever appropriate.

As always please refer to the tablature for fret and string placement. This eliminates a lot of the clutter in the manuscript and allows for easy and smooth reading. When necessary, I added fingering into the manuscript itself.

The recording of these arrangements was done on a nylon string guitar, but they are suited to both nylon and steel string guitar equally and should be easily accessible to the intermediate guitarist.

I am really drawn to the unexpected and asymmetrical melodic phrases and unusual harmonic resolutions of this era. I found in creating these arrangements that the music felt very fluid which should make it very comfortable for either sight reading or learning a few together as a performance collection.

All the best,
Raymond

Contents

1

Adoro Devote

⑥ = D

Freely

13th Century Plainsong
arr. Raymond Gonzalez

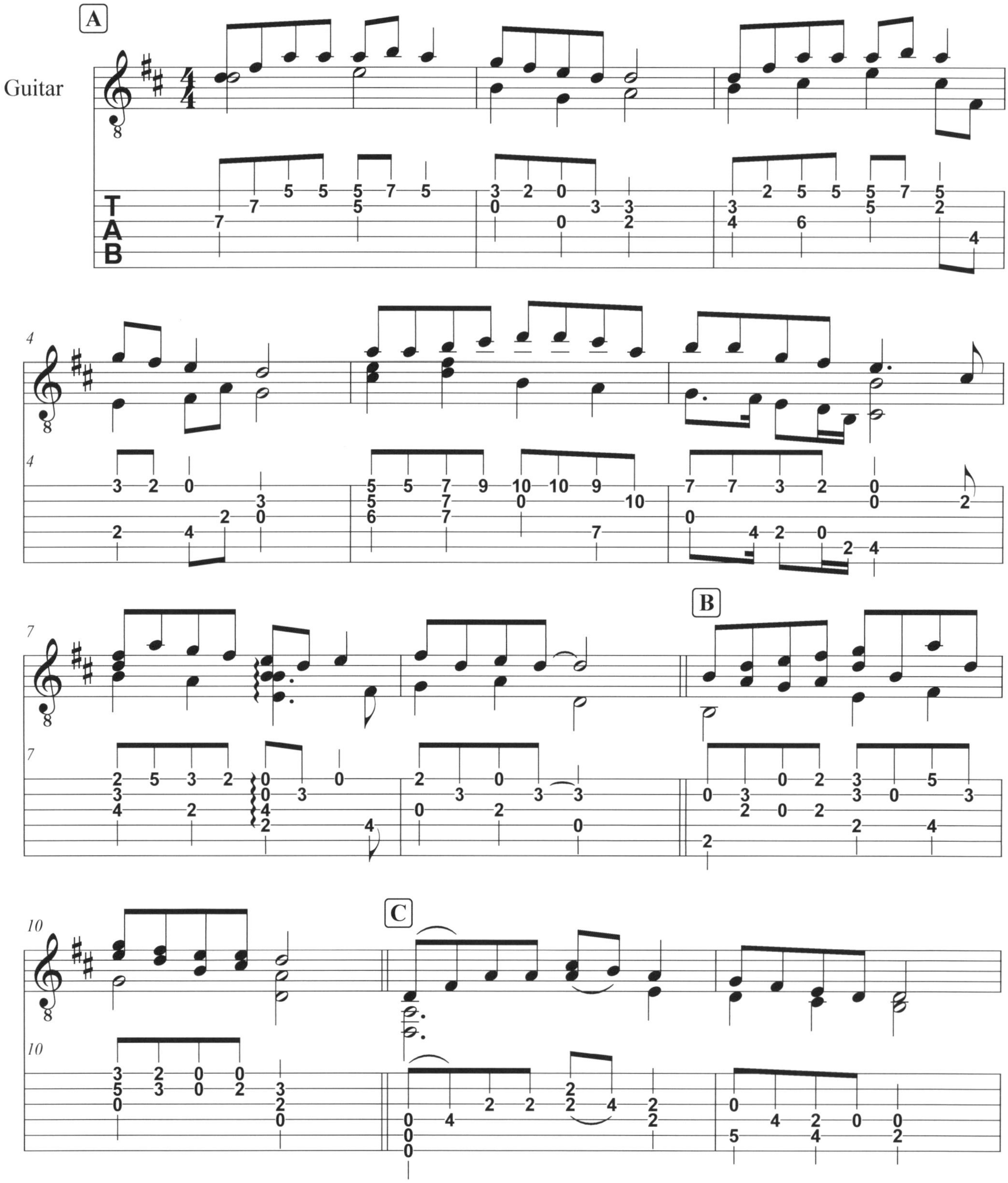

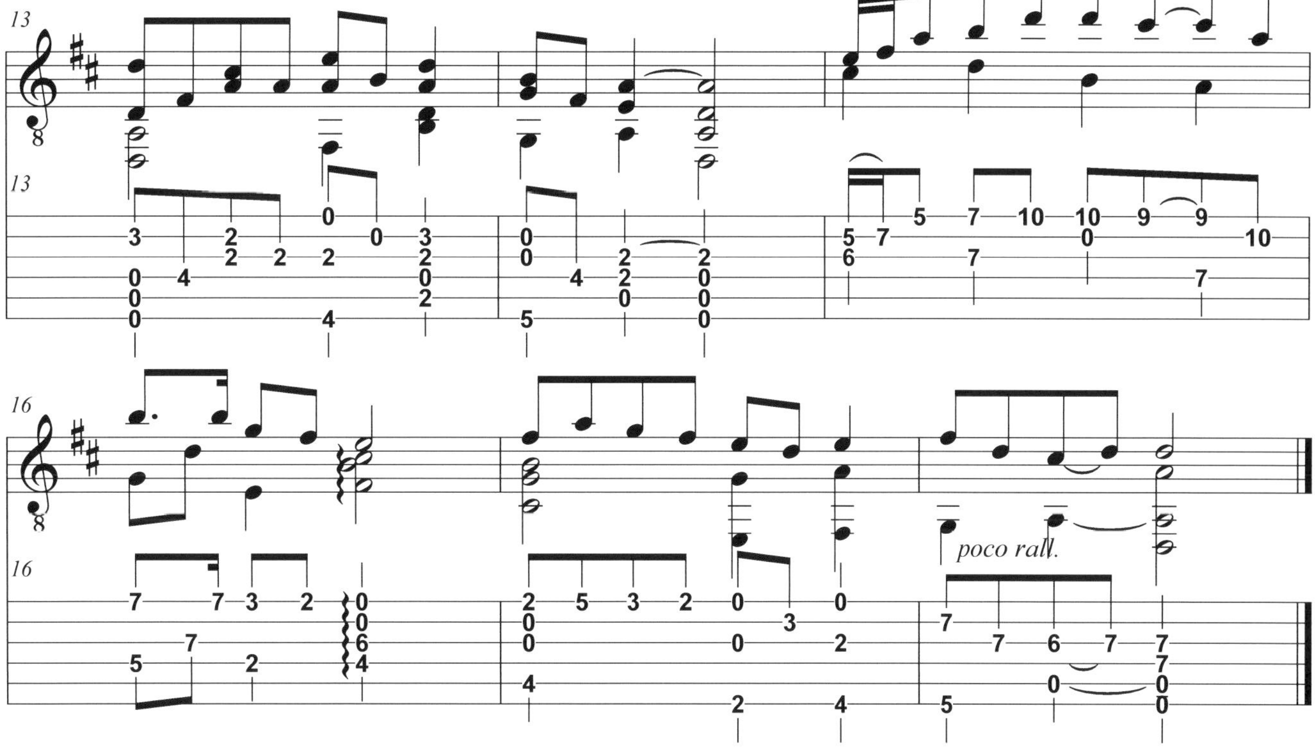
poco rall.

Allegro

⑥ = D

Anonymous
arr. Raymond Gonzalez

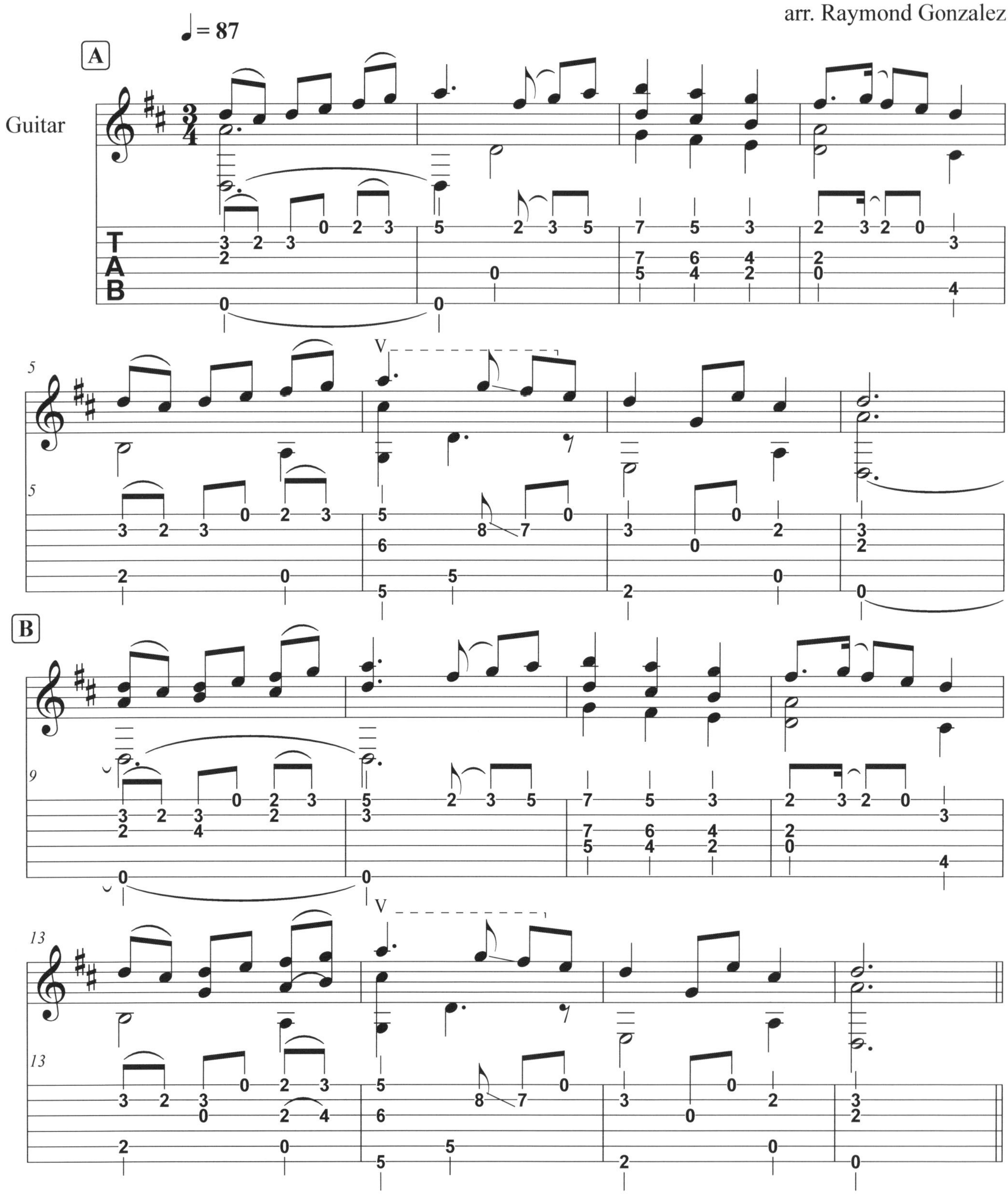

C

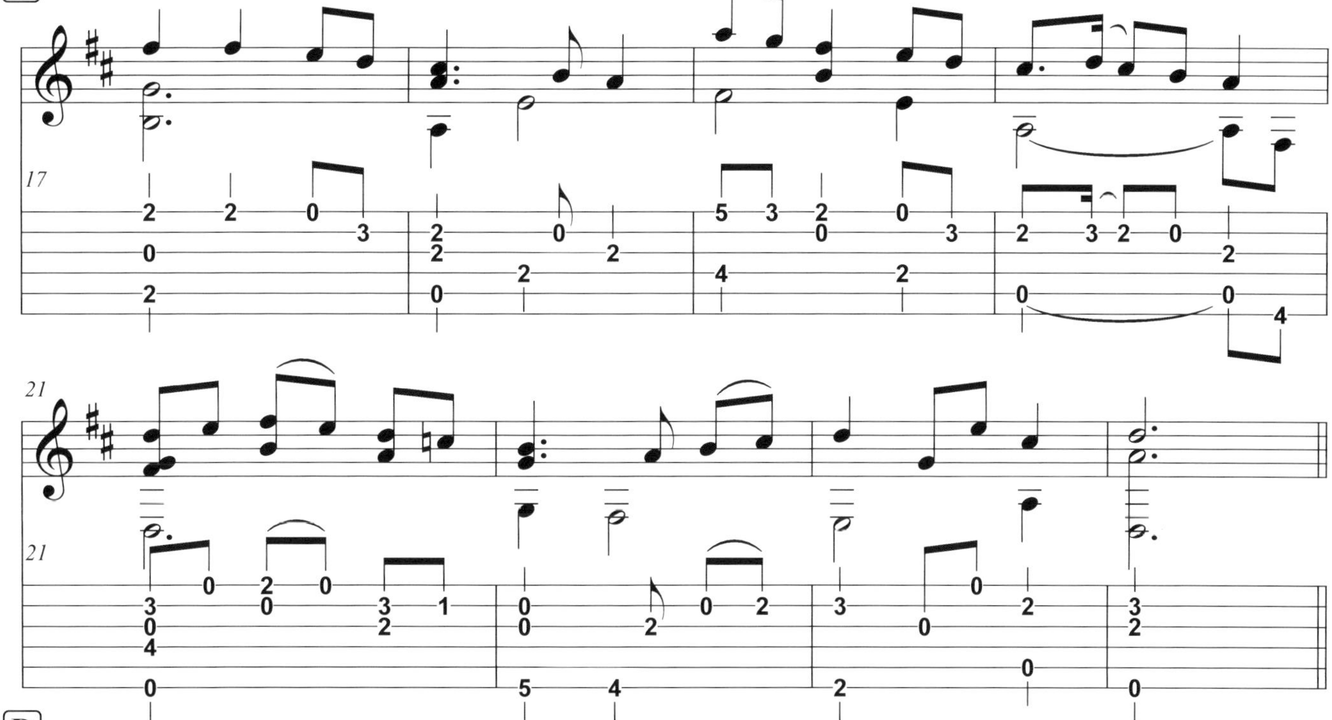

D

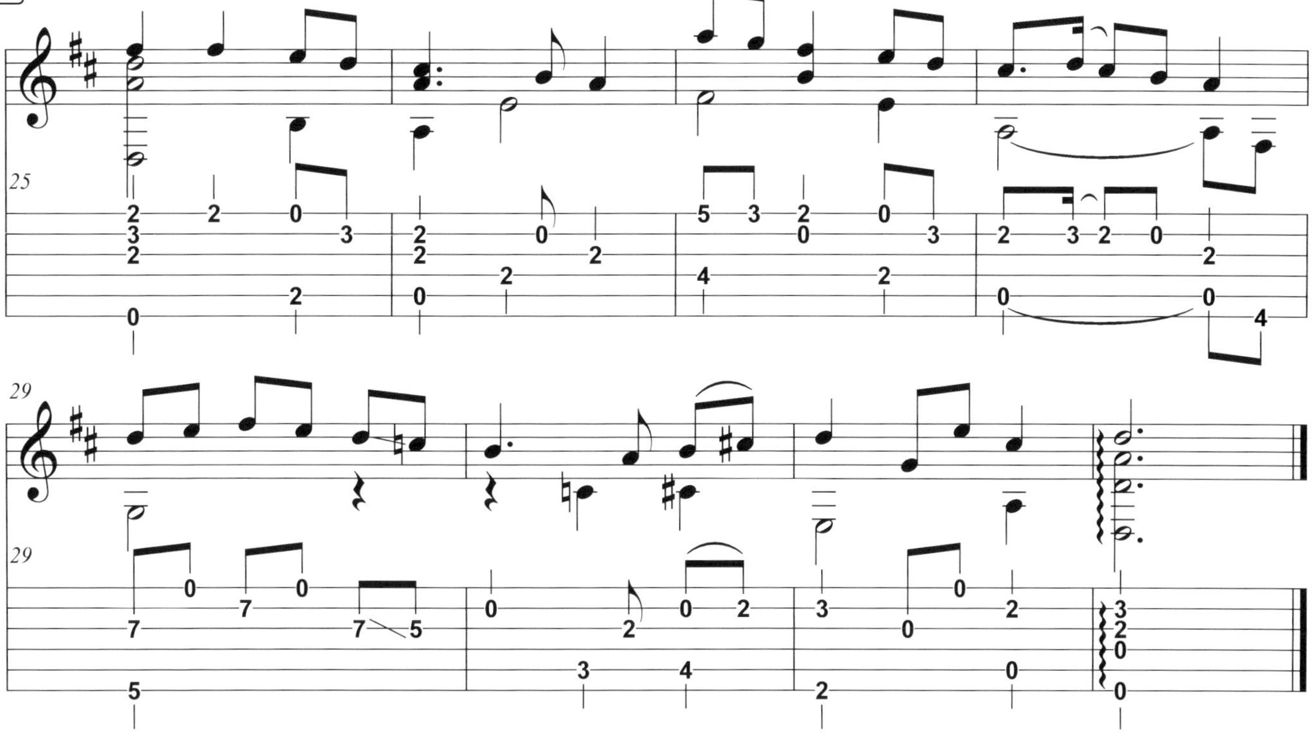

Alman

Robert Johnson
arr. Raymond Gonzalez

♩ = 100

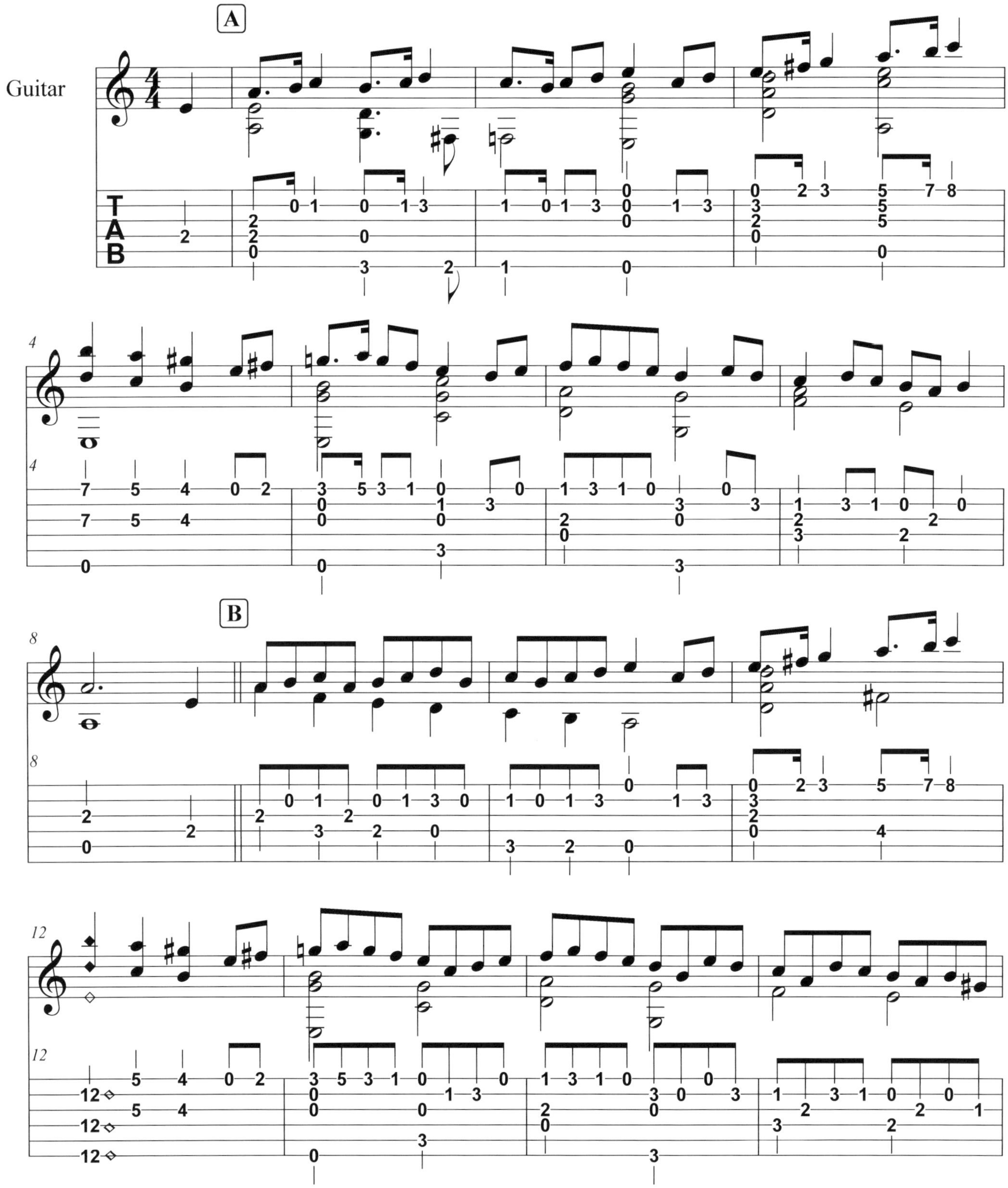

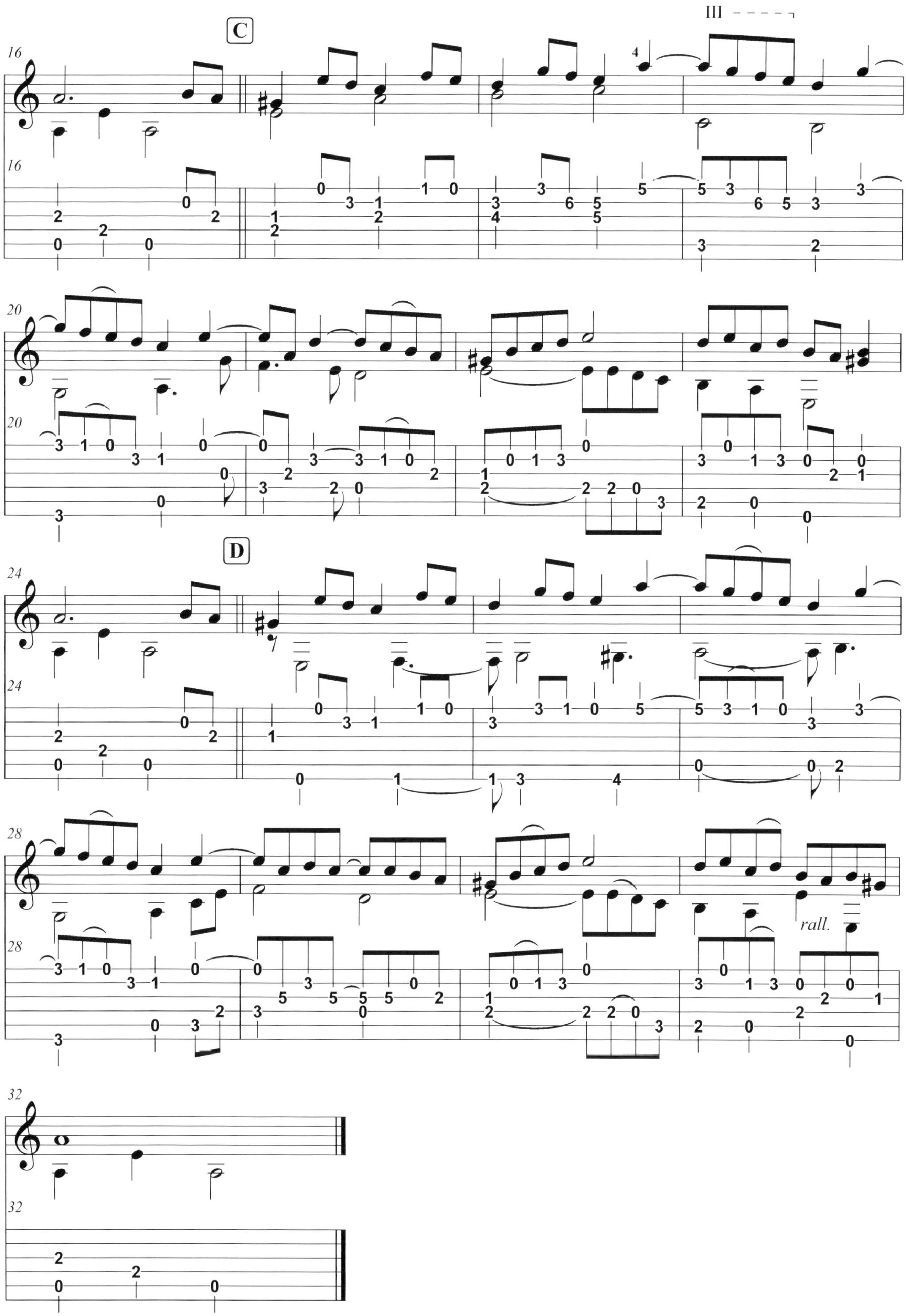
C
III
D
rall.

4

An Italian Rant

♩ = 80 Freely

John Playford
arr. Raymond Gonzalez

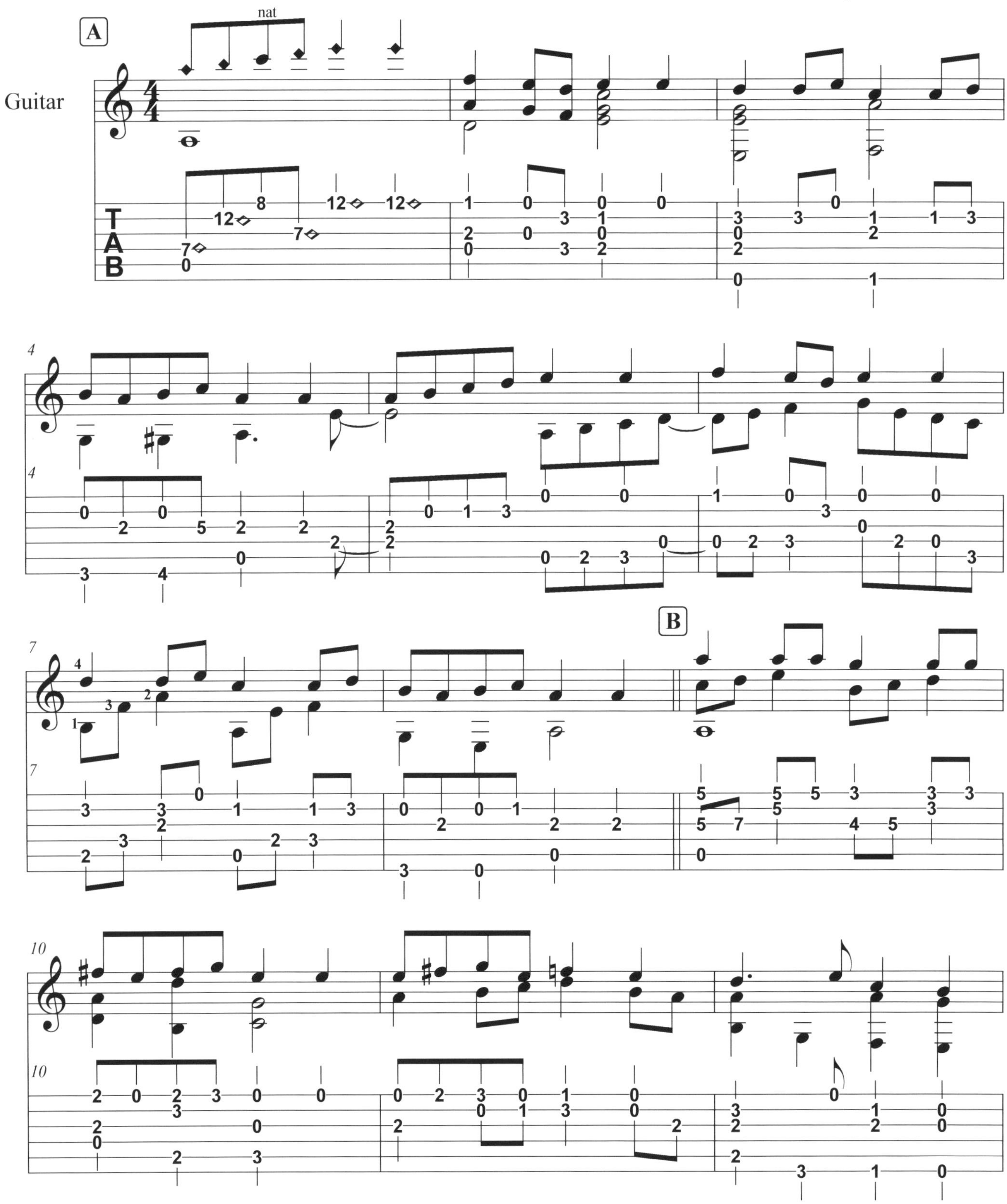

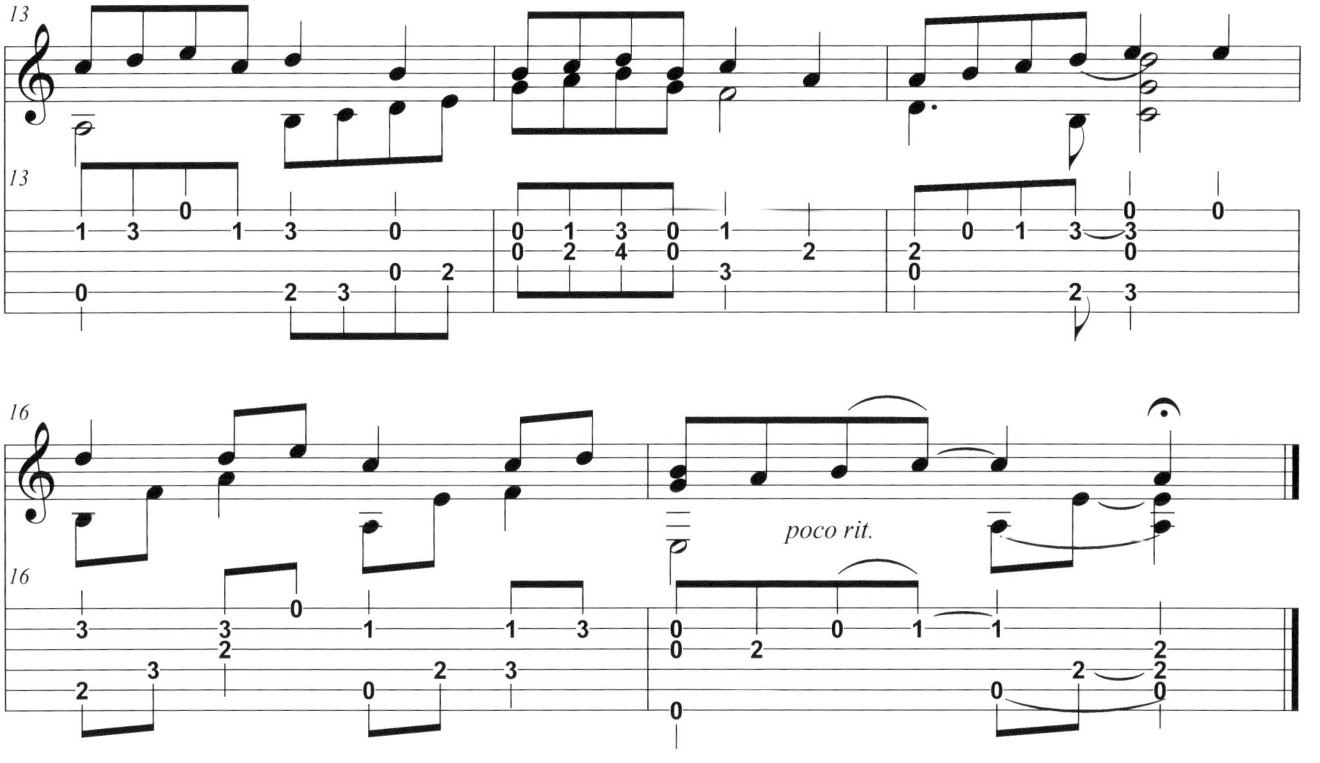
poco rit.

Andante

⑥ = D

Anonymous
arr. Raymond Gonzalez

Gracefully

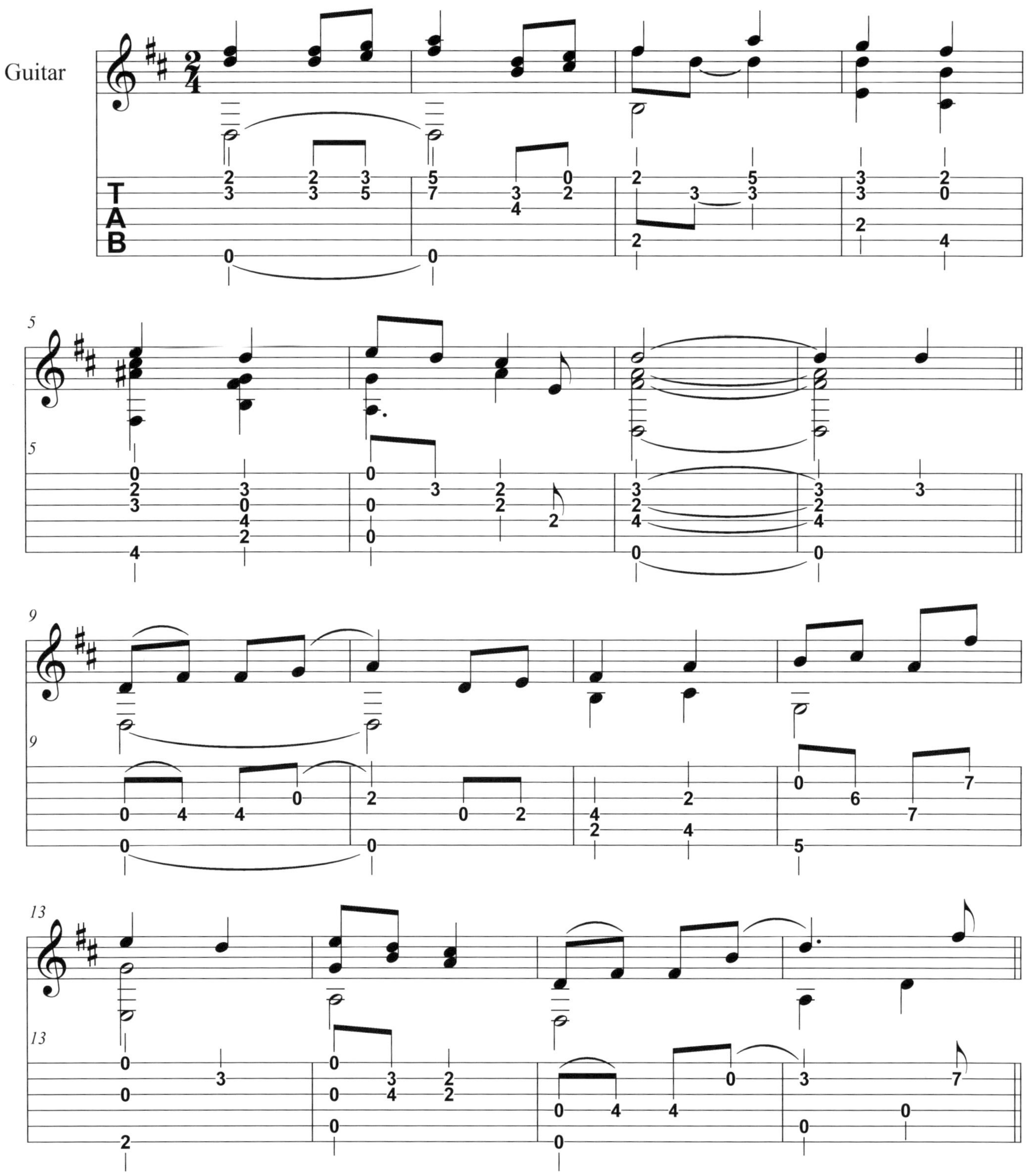

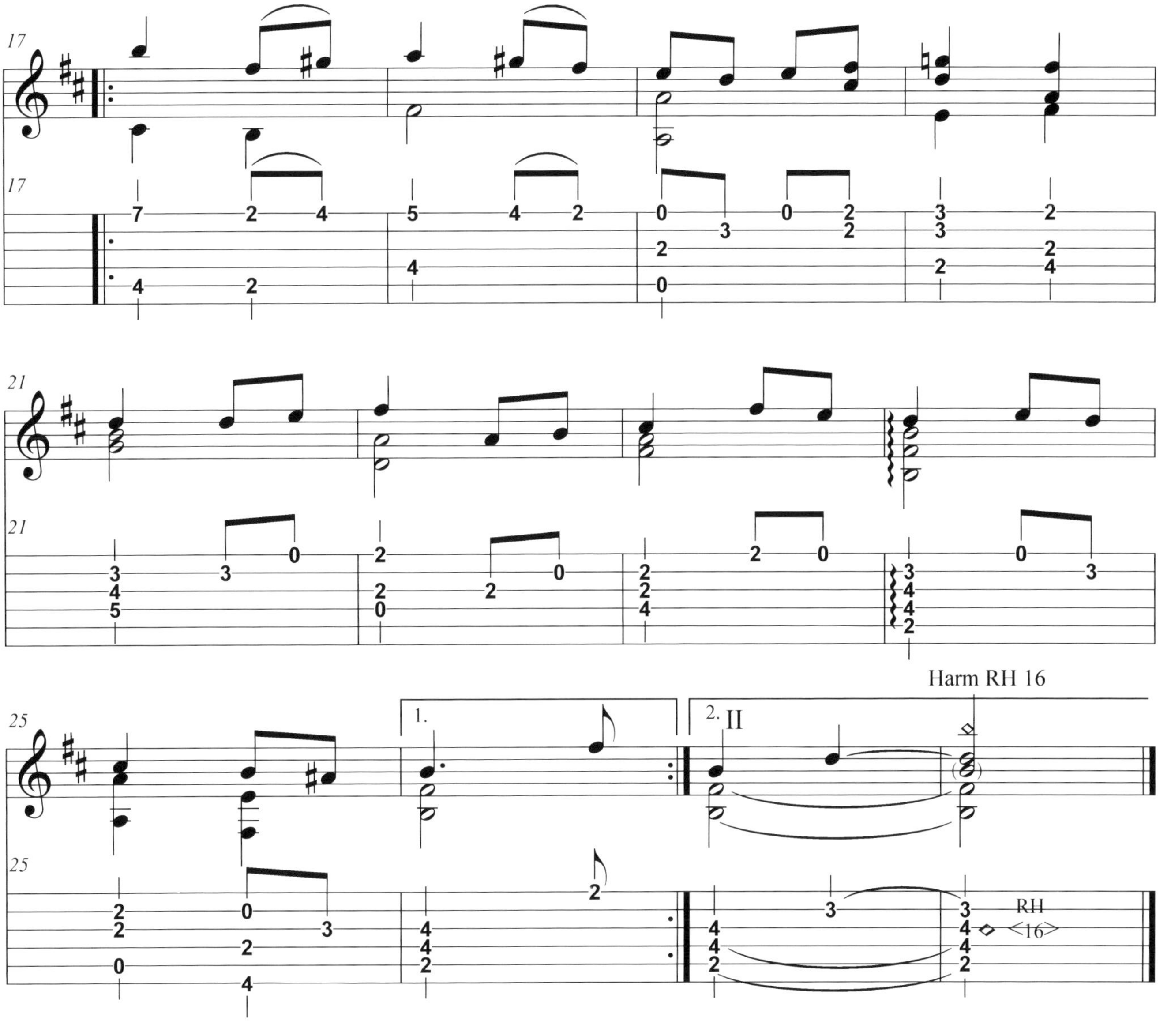

Harm RH 16
II
RH
<16>

Ballade

⑥ = D

Adagio ♩ = 68

Anonymous
arr. Raymond Gonzalez

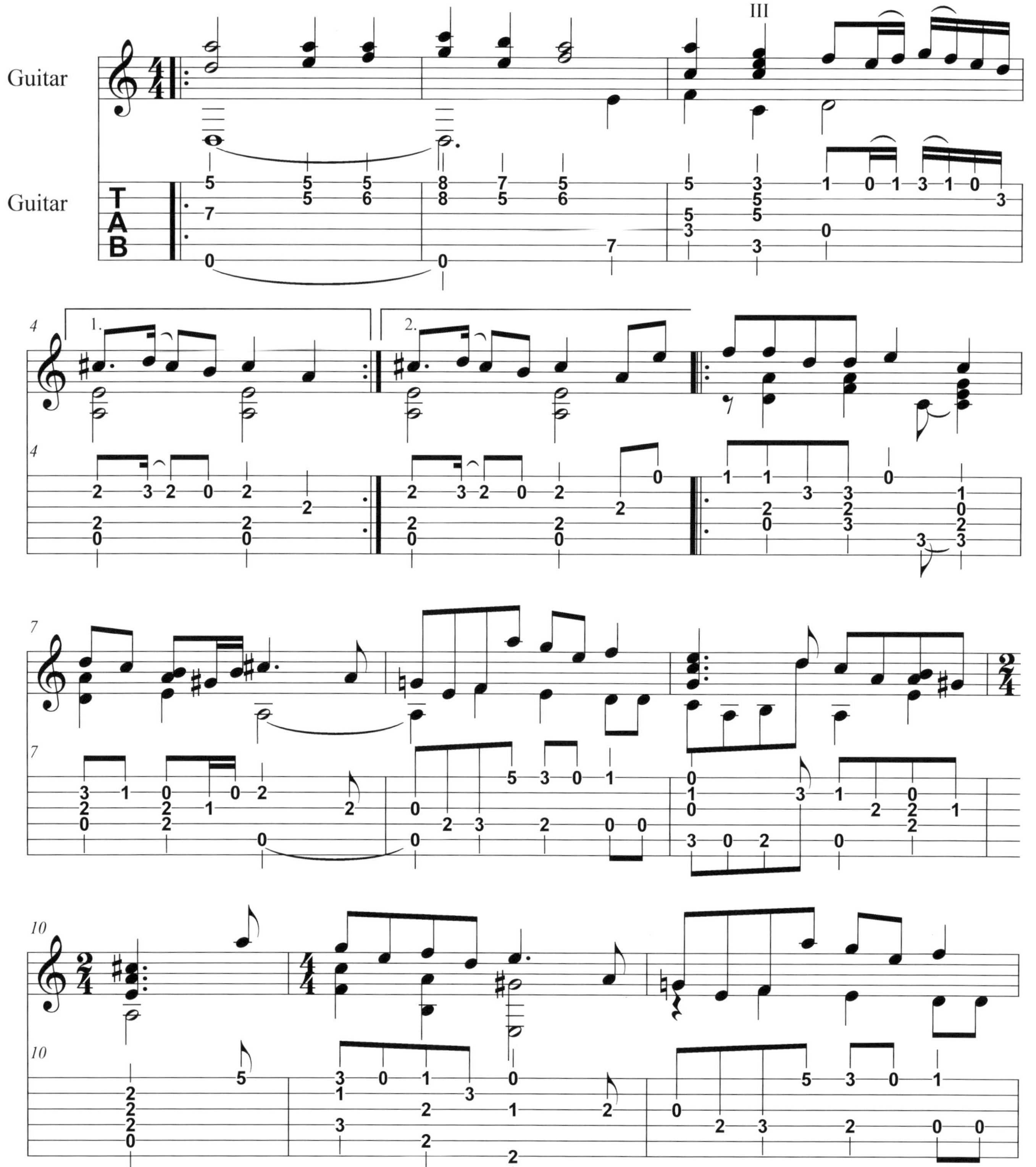

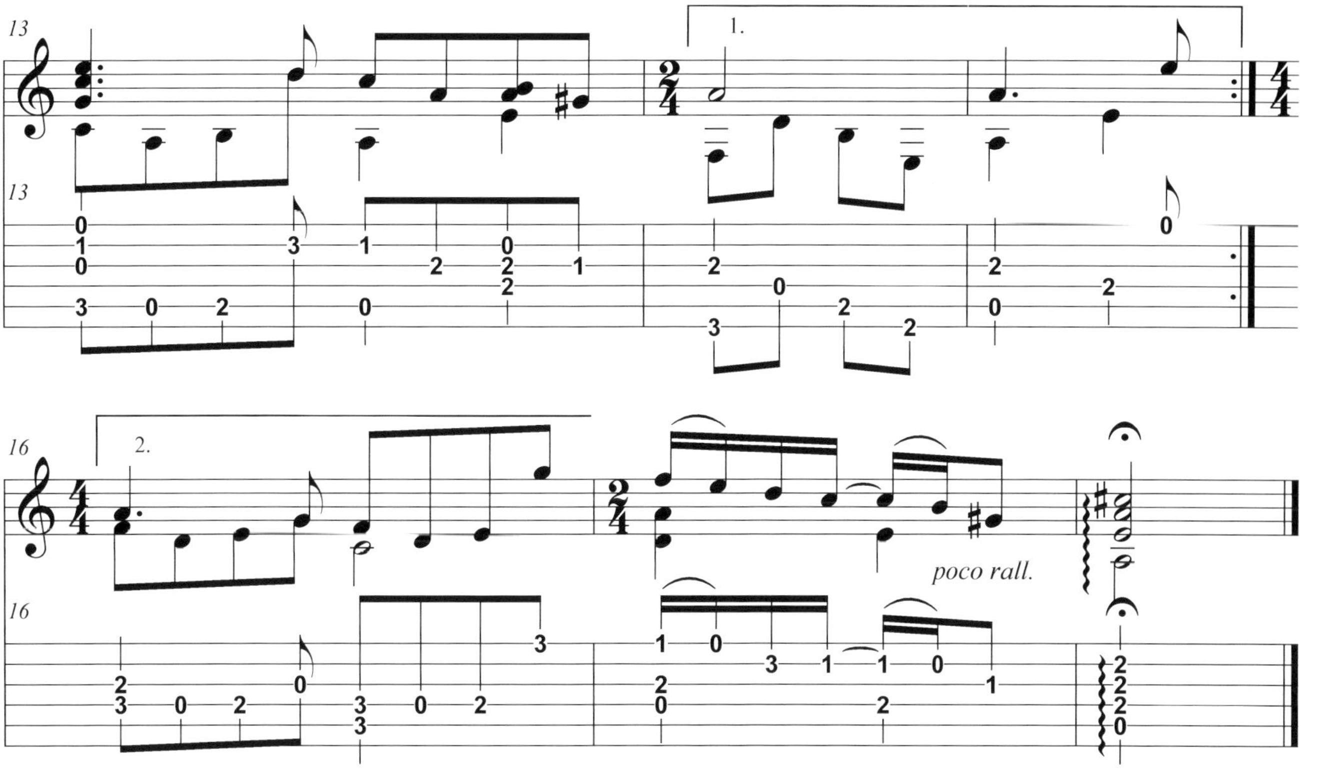
13
1.
16
2.
poco rall.

7

Bear Dance

Moderate ♩ = **82**

arr. Raymond Gonzalez

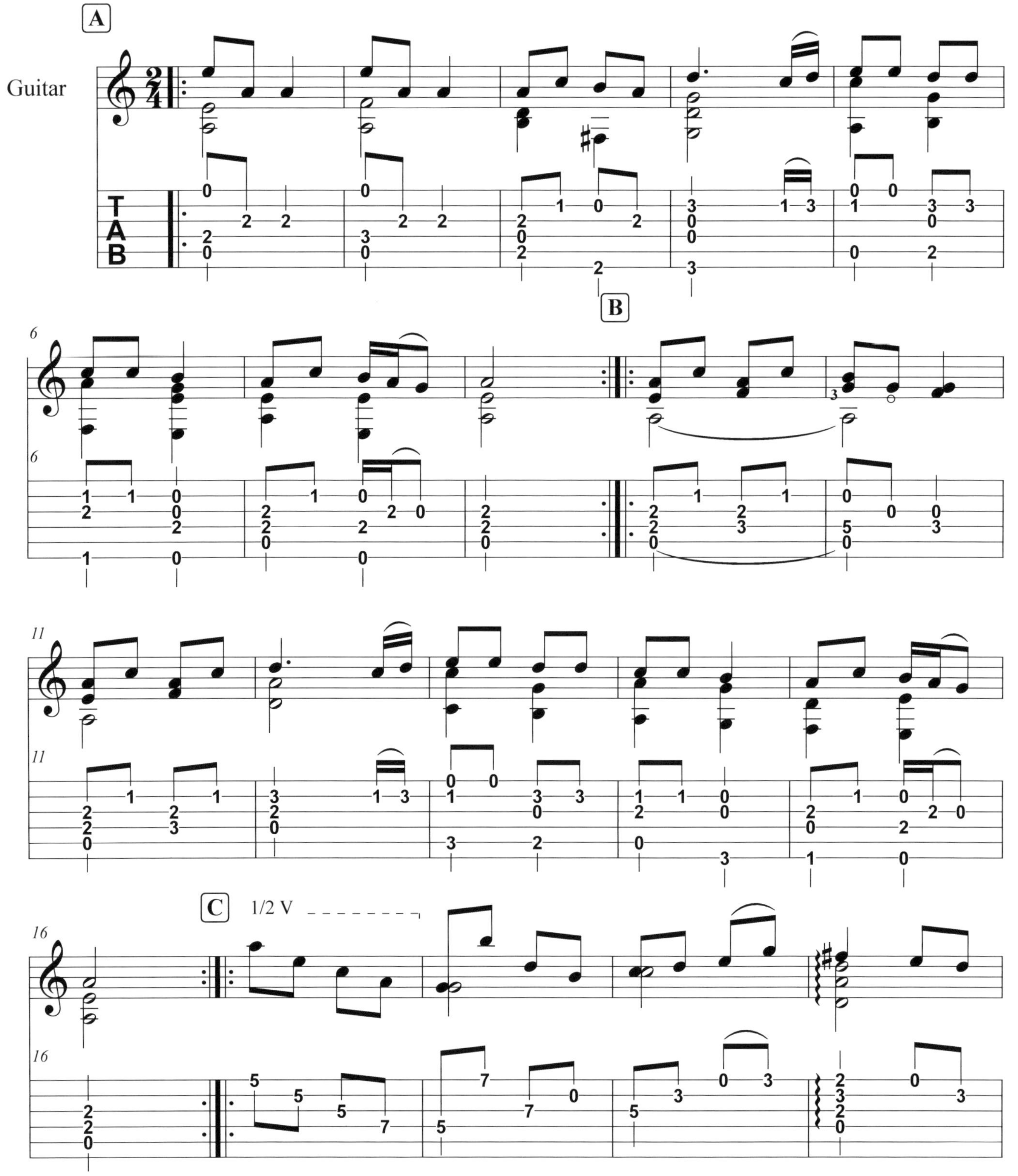

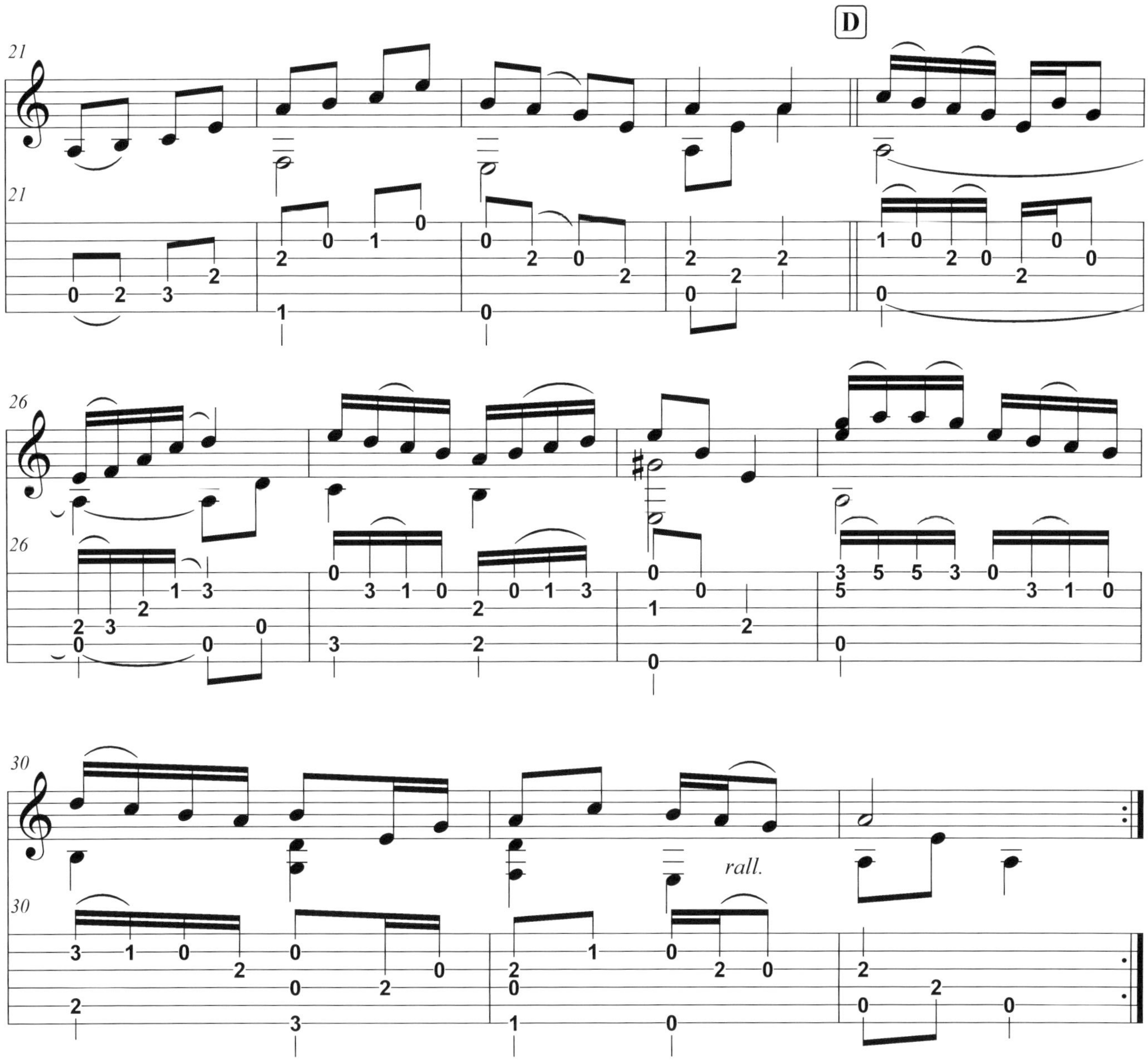
D
rall.

8

Branle Double

Michael Praetorious
arr. Raymond Gonzalez

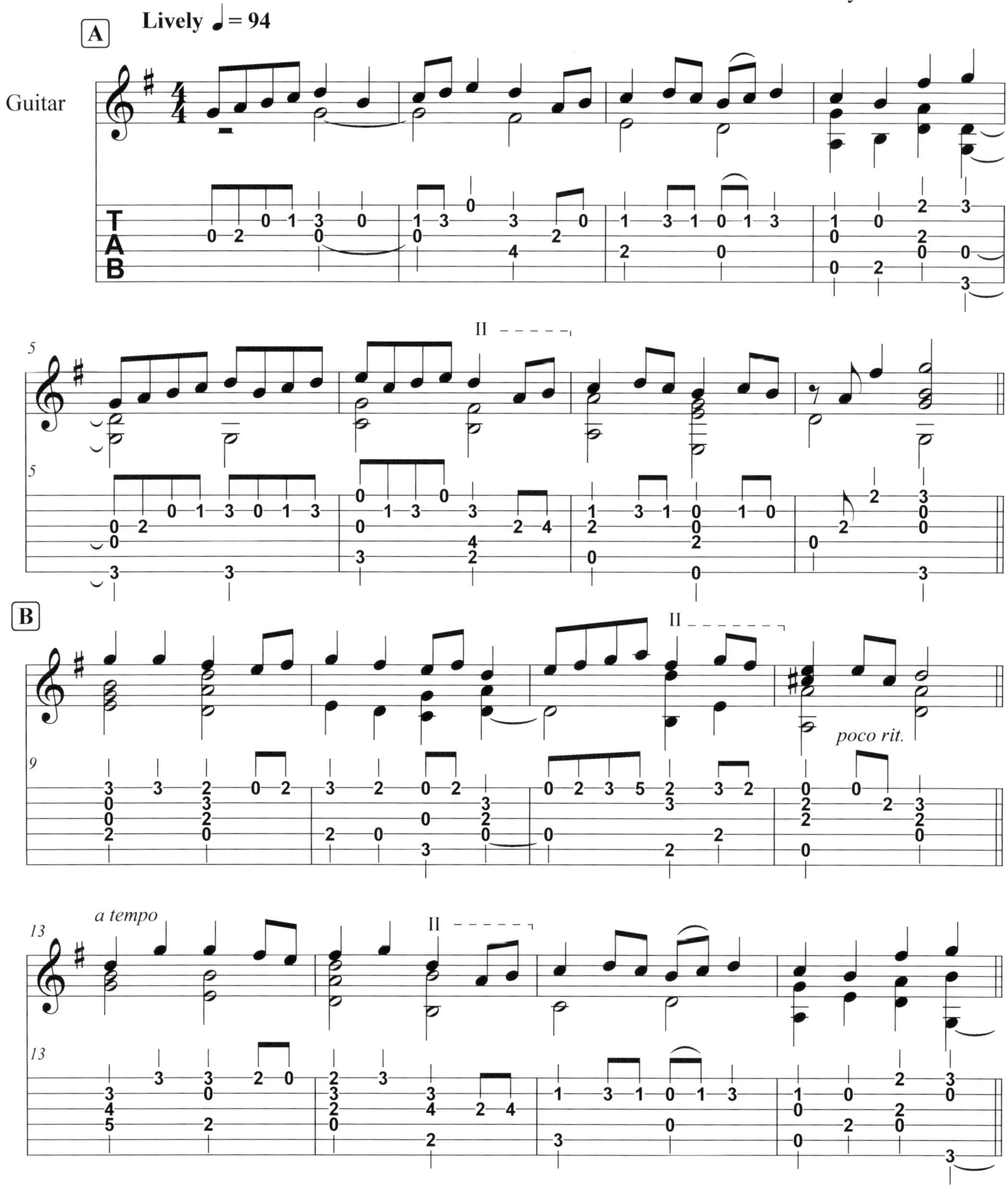

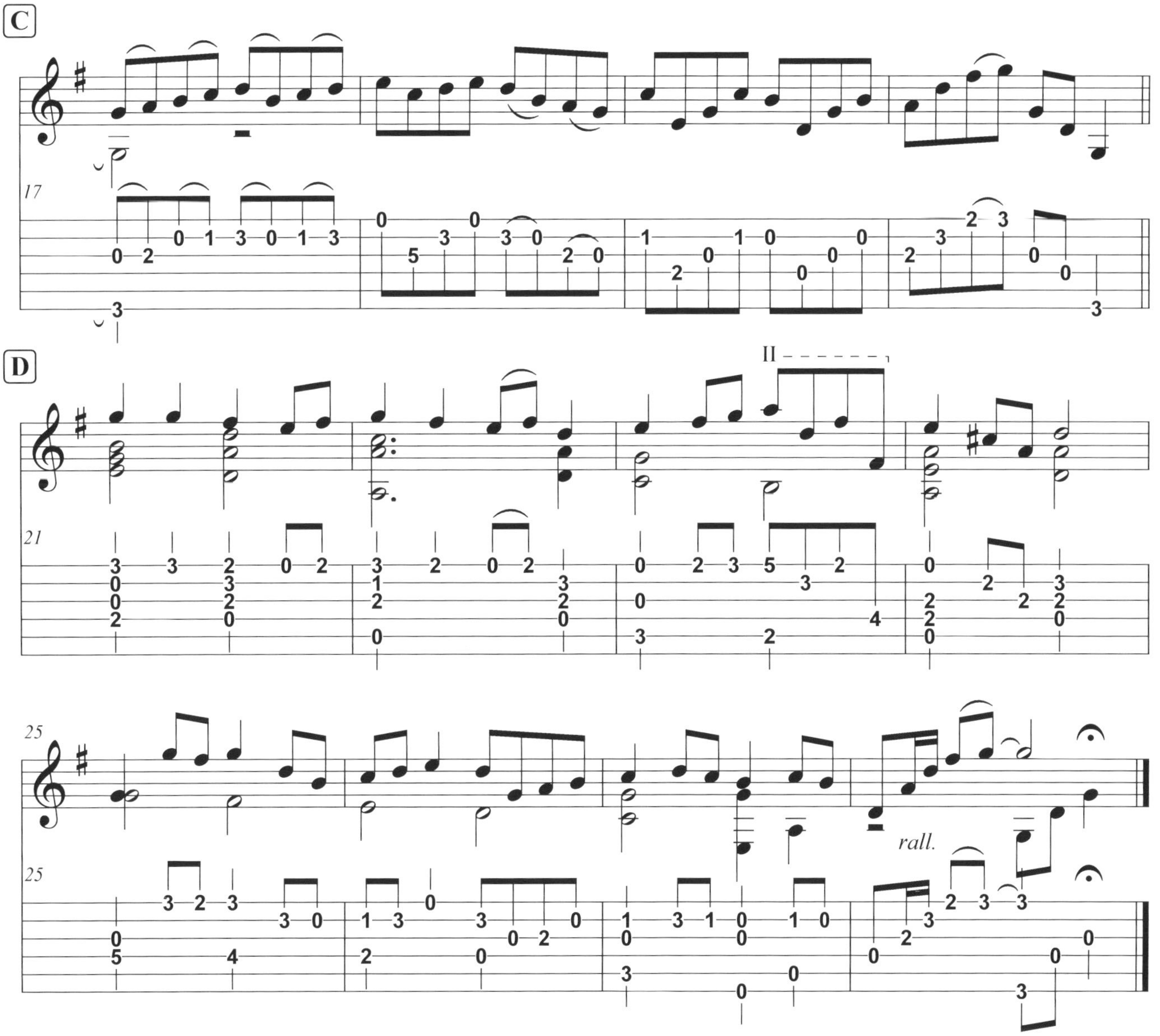
C
D
II
rall.

Canarios

Gaspar Sanz
arr. Raymond Gonzalez

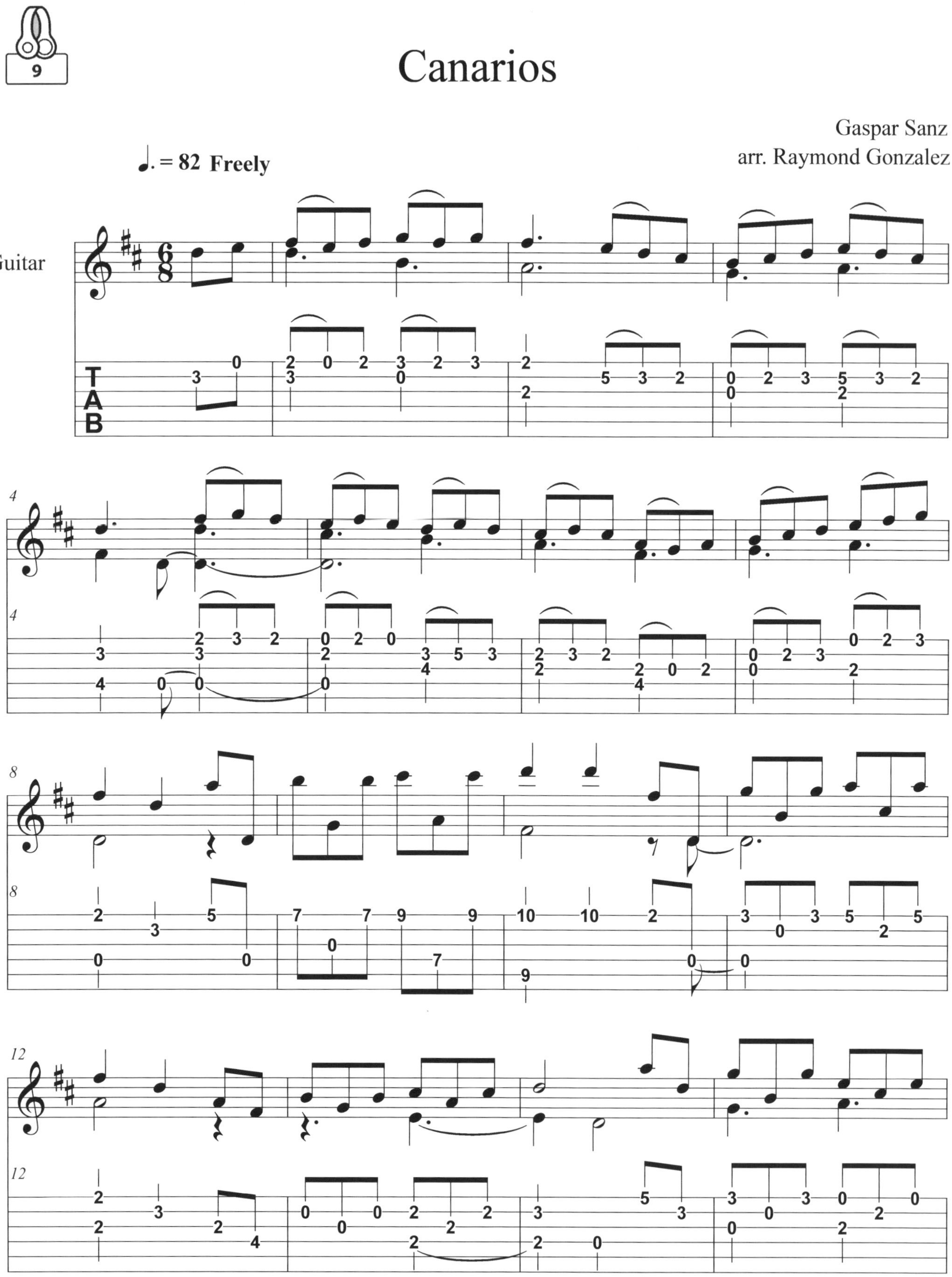

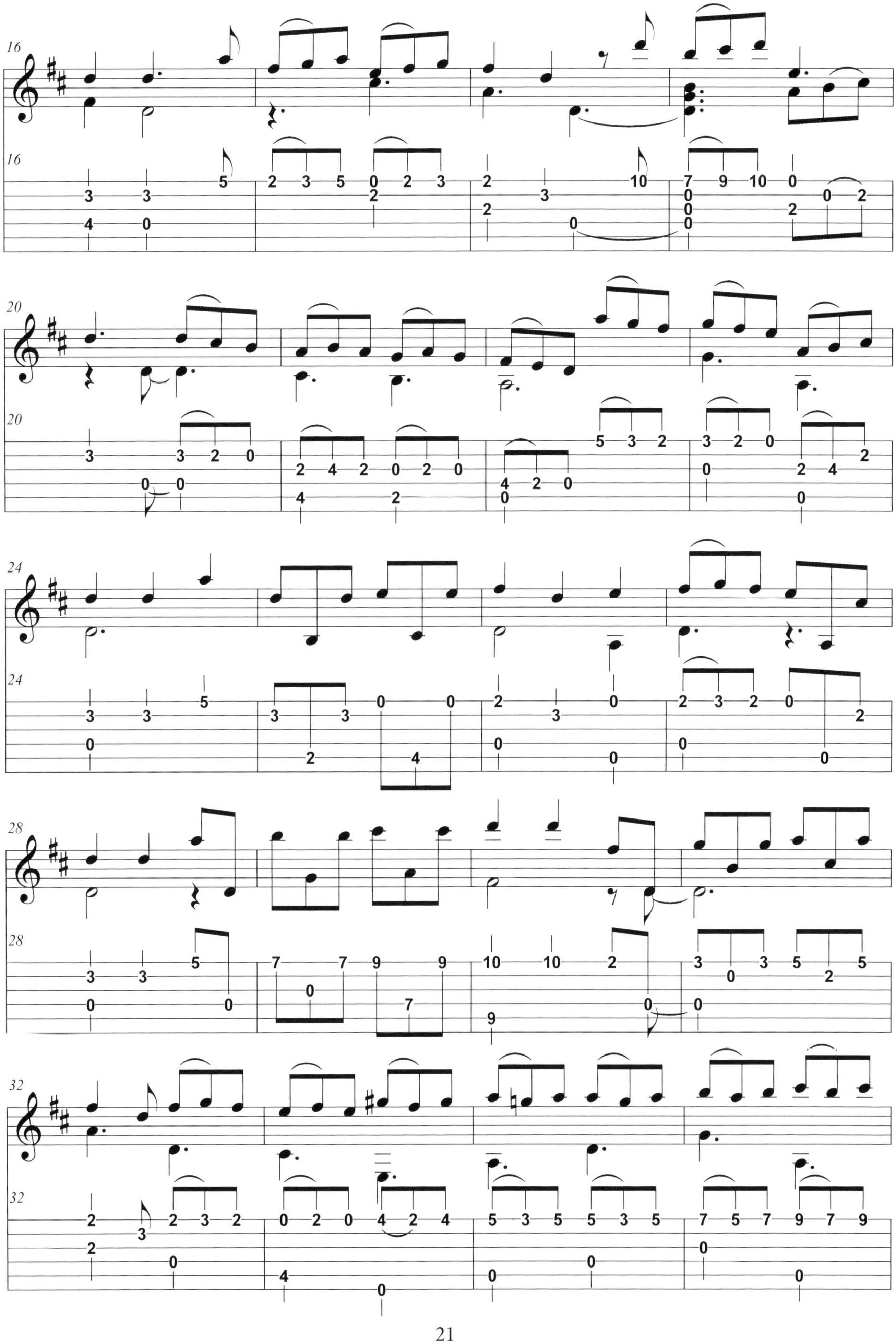

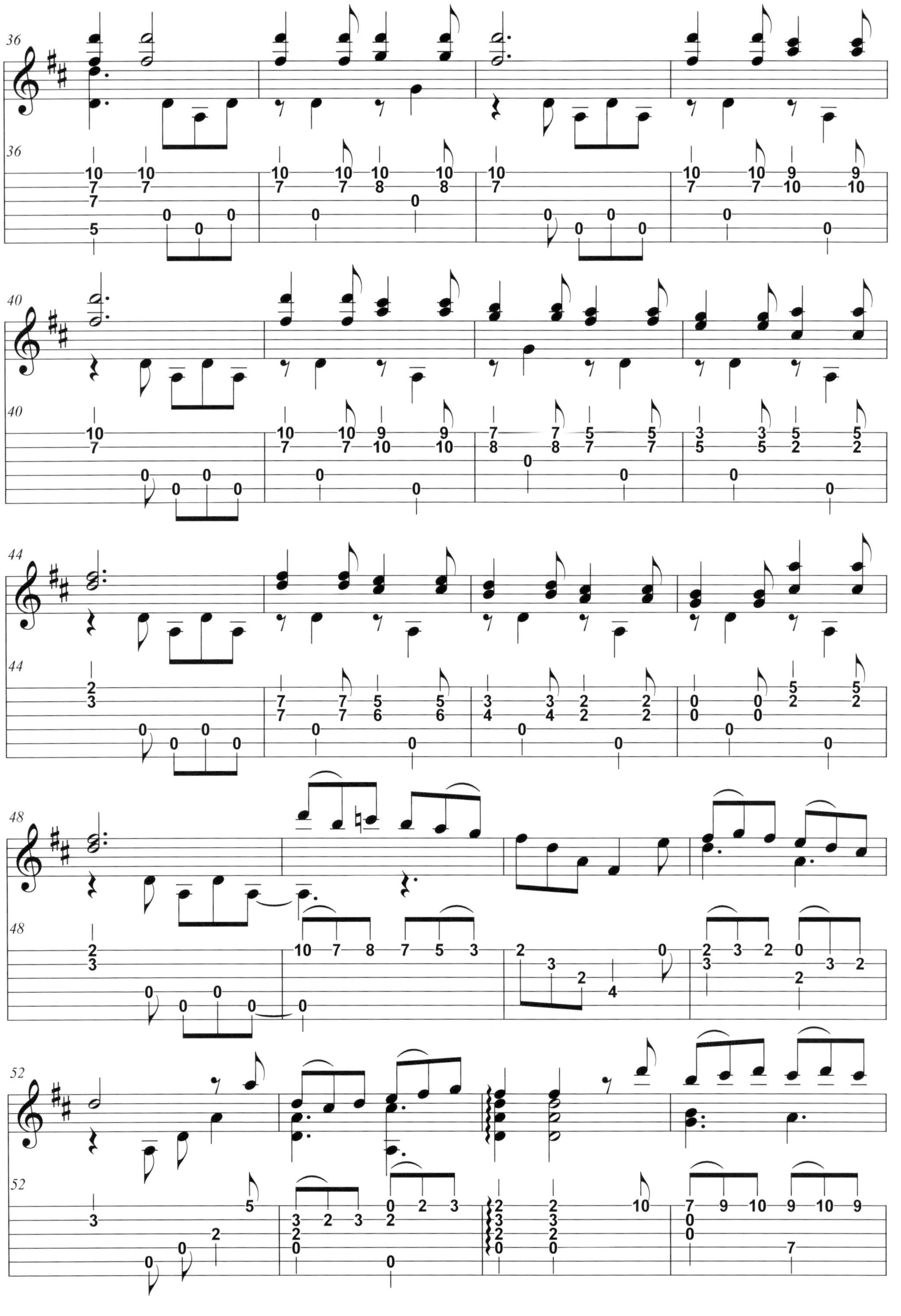

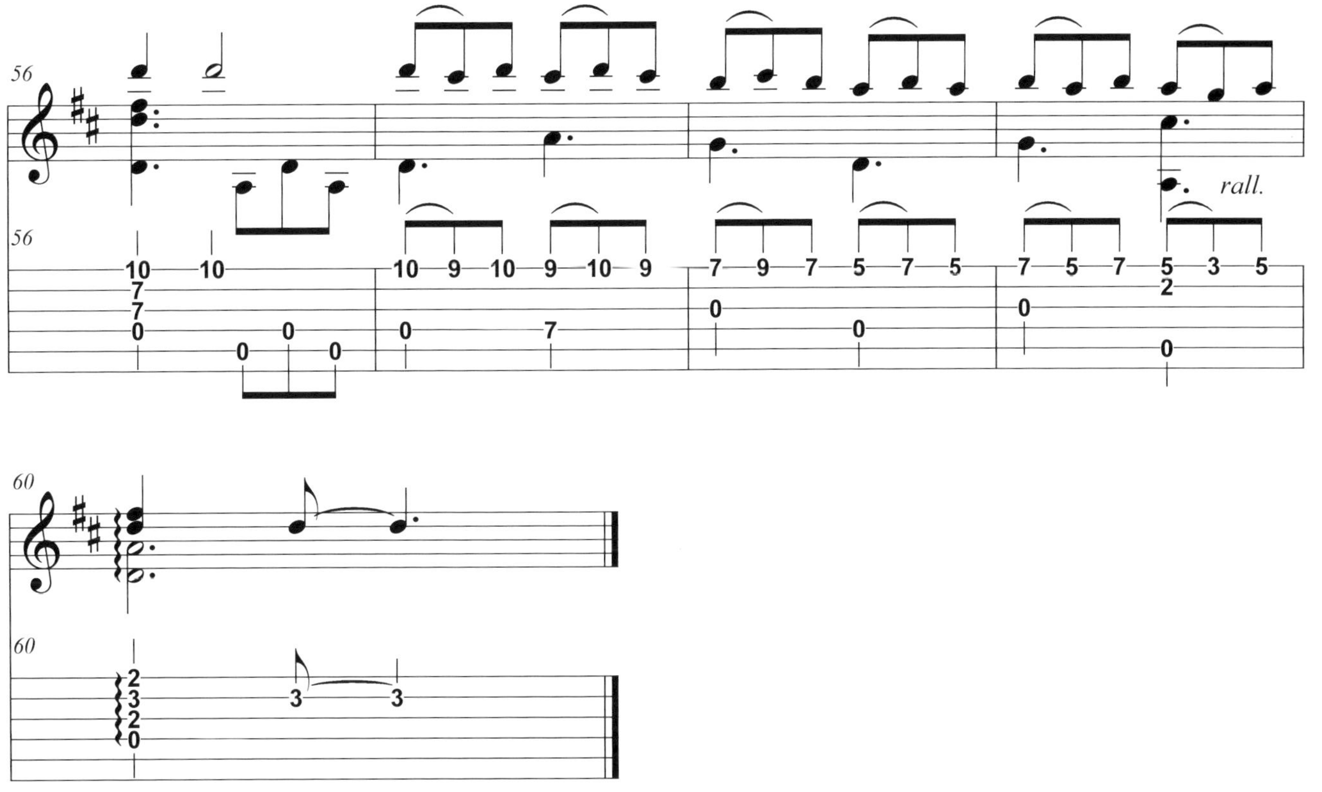
56
rall.
60

10

Childgrove

Playford Collection
arr. Raymond Gonzalez

𝅗𝅥 = 70

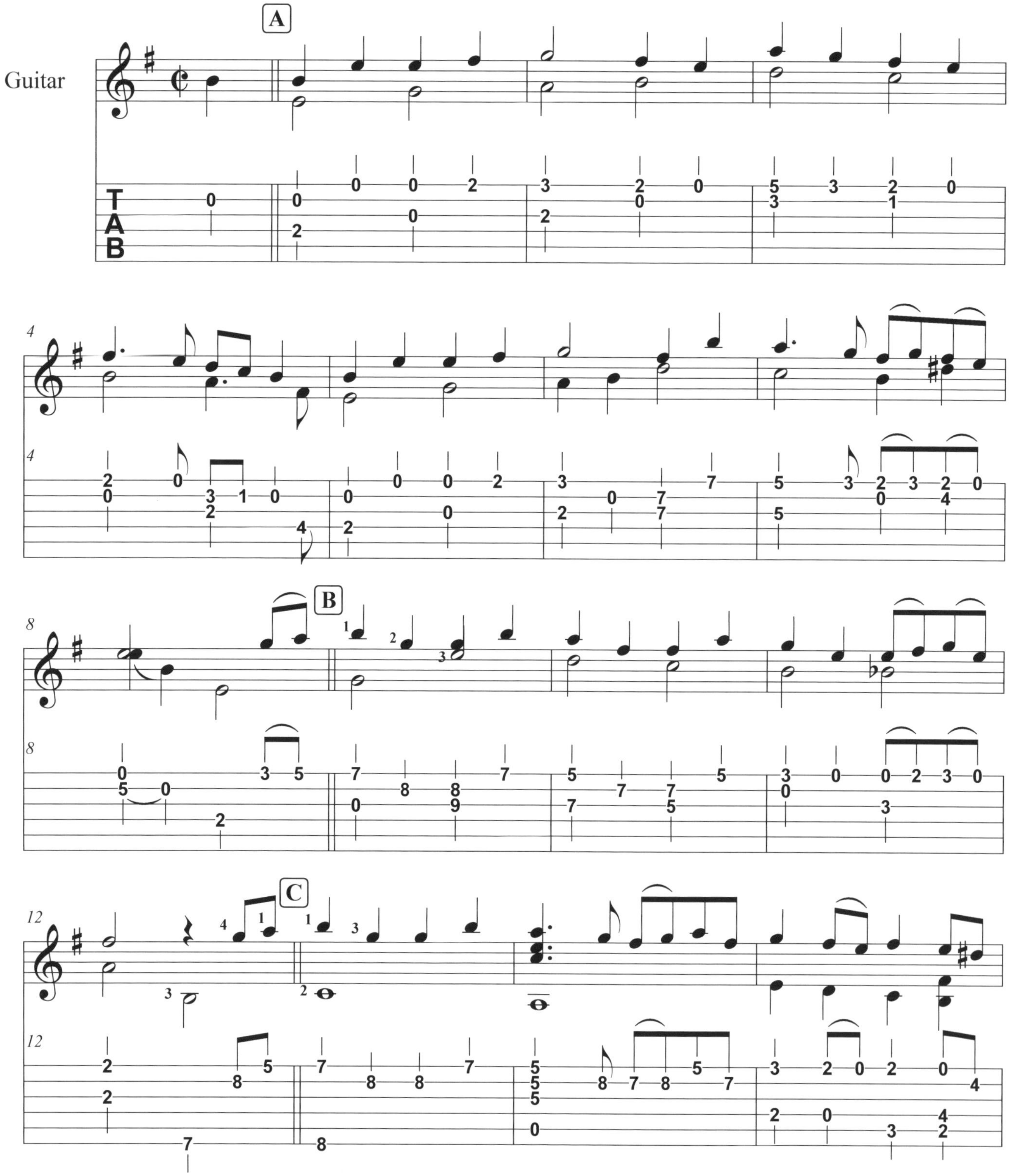

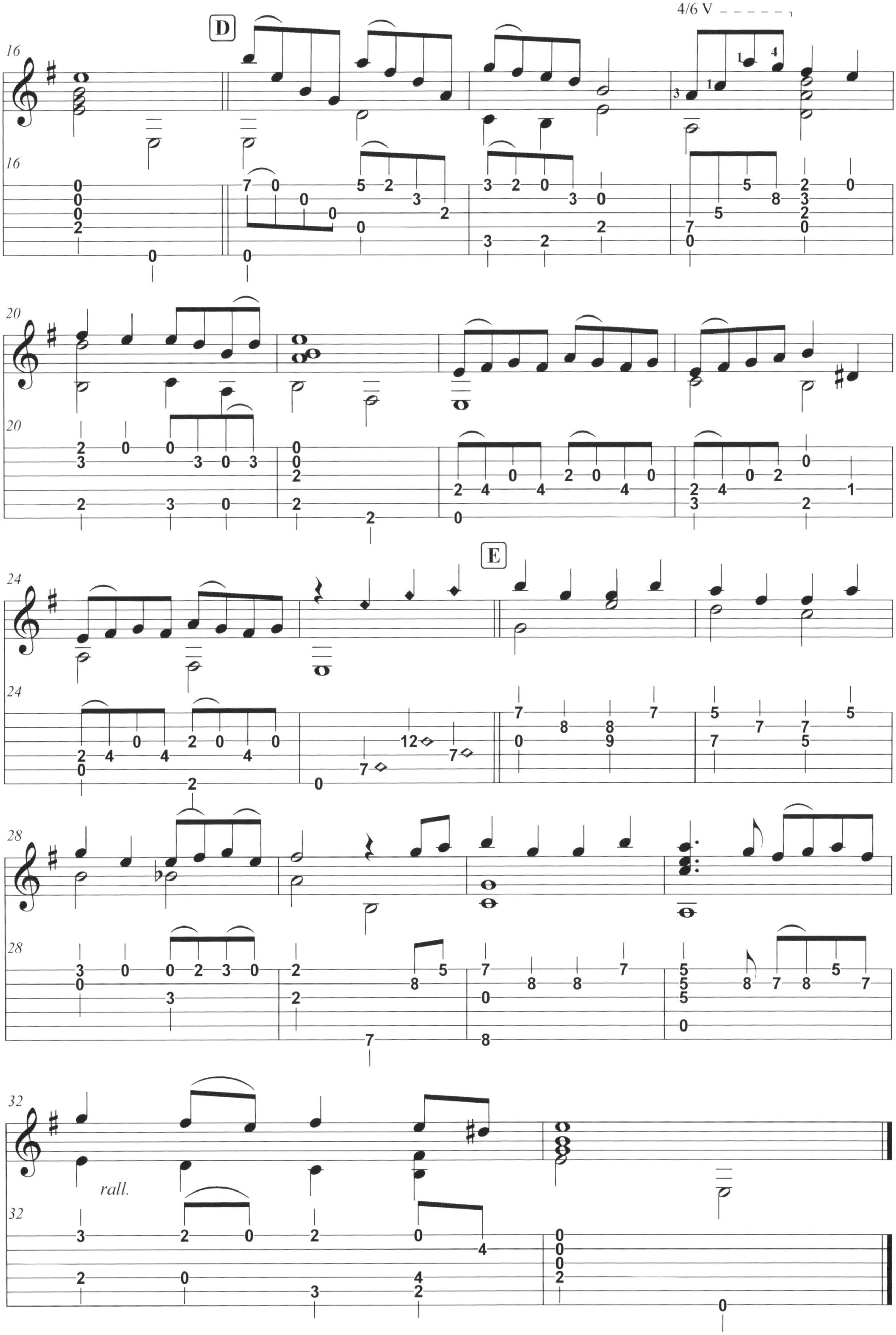
D
4/6 V
E
rall.

11

Come With Me, My Giselle

Adam de la Halle
arr. Raymond Gonzalez

Andante ♩ = 76

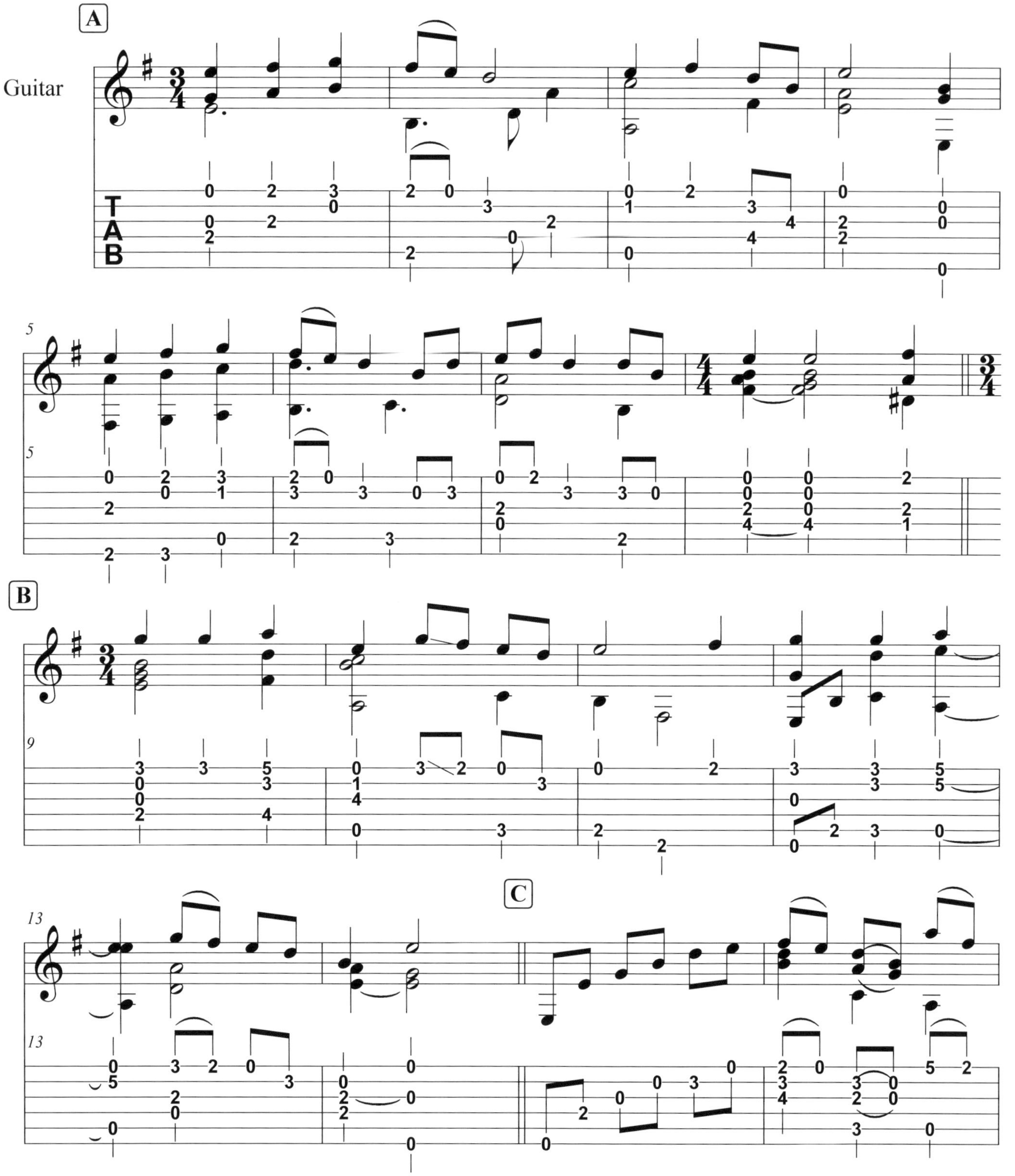

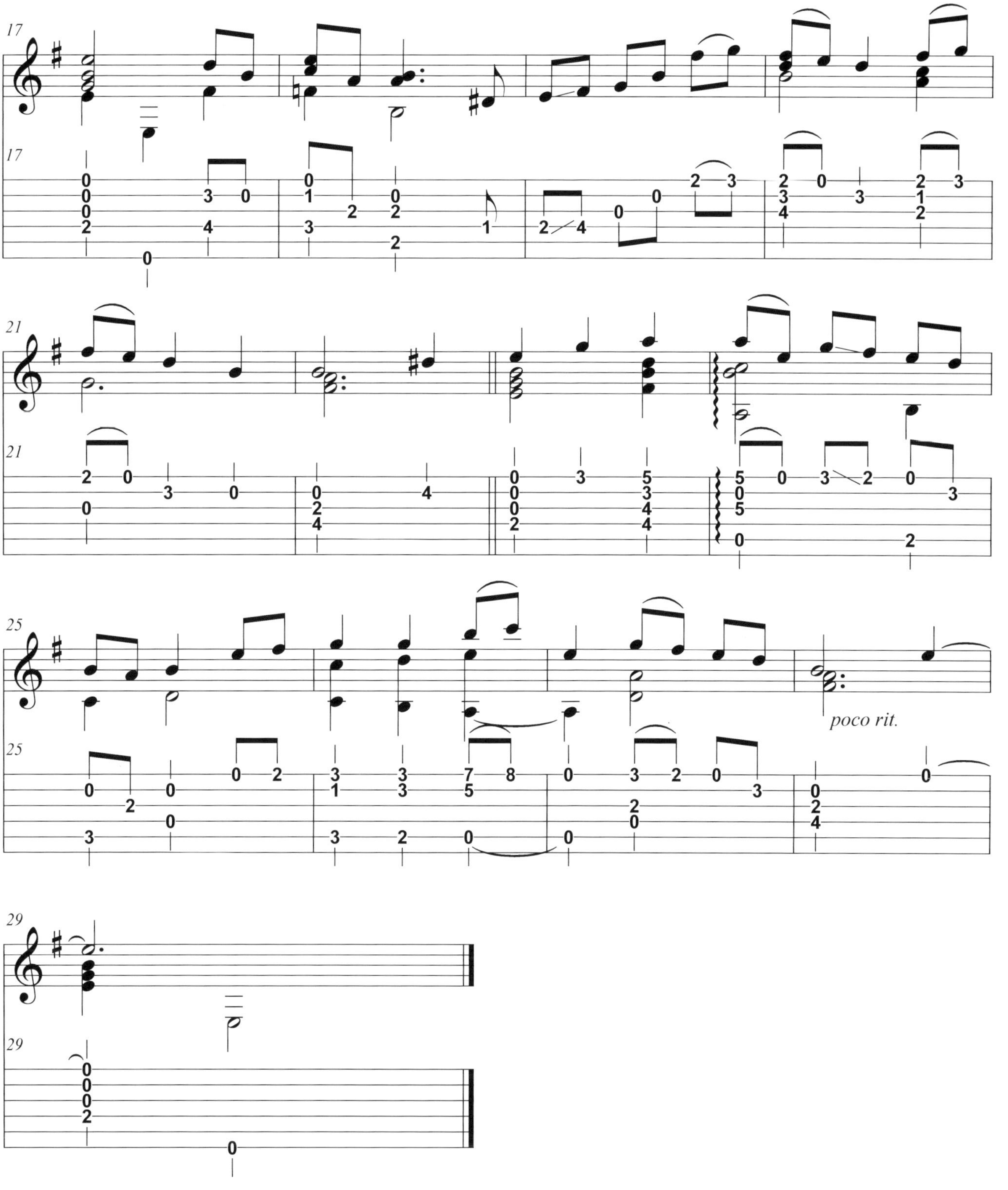
poco rit.

12

Dont vient cela

Susato Danserye 1551
arr. Raymond Gonzalez

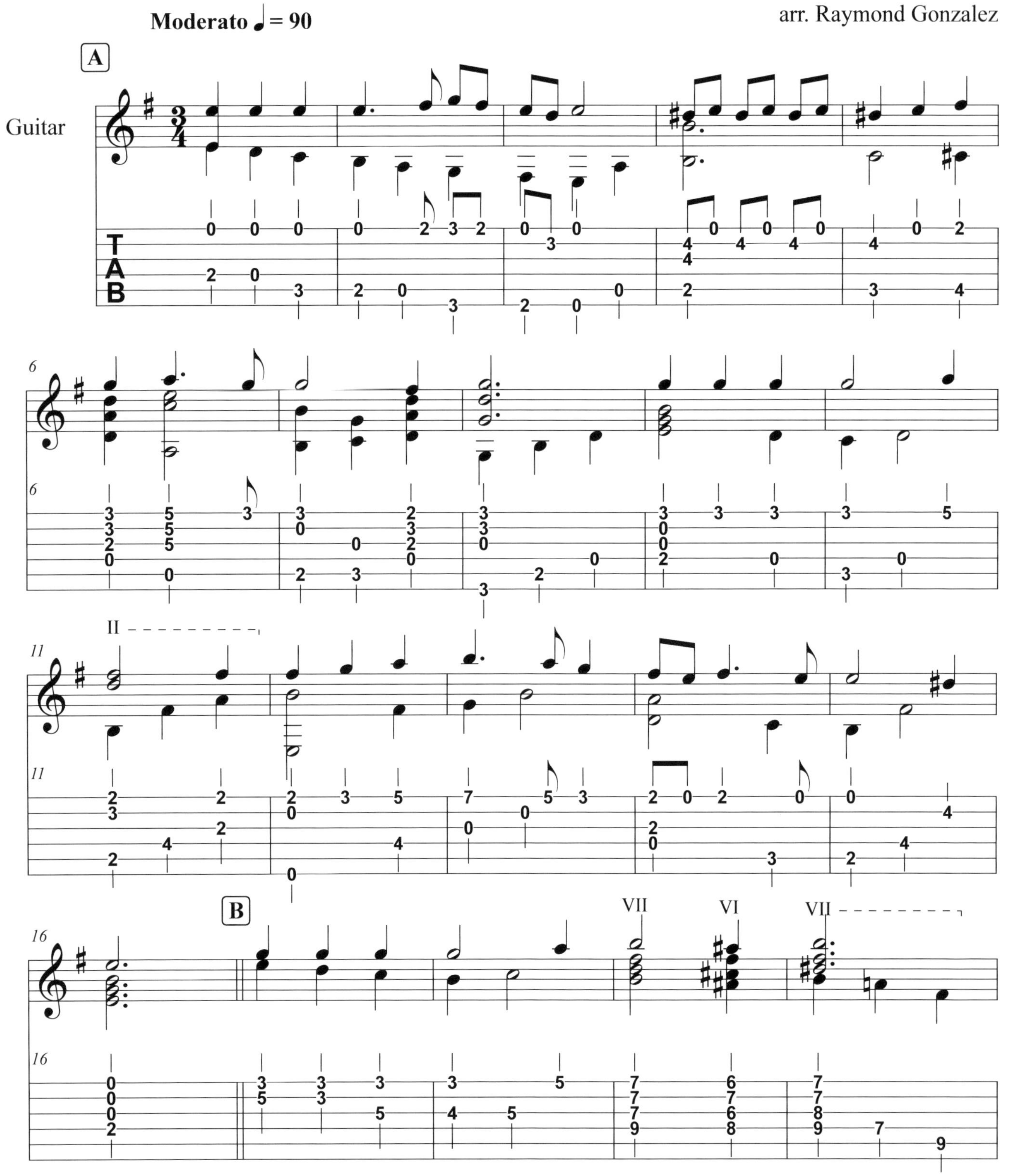

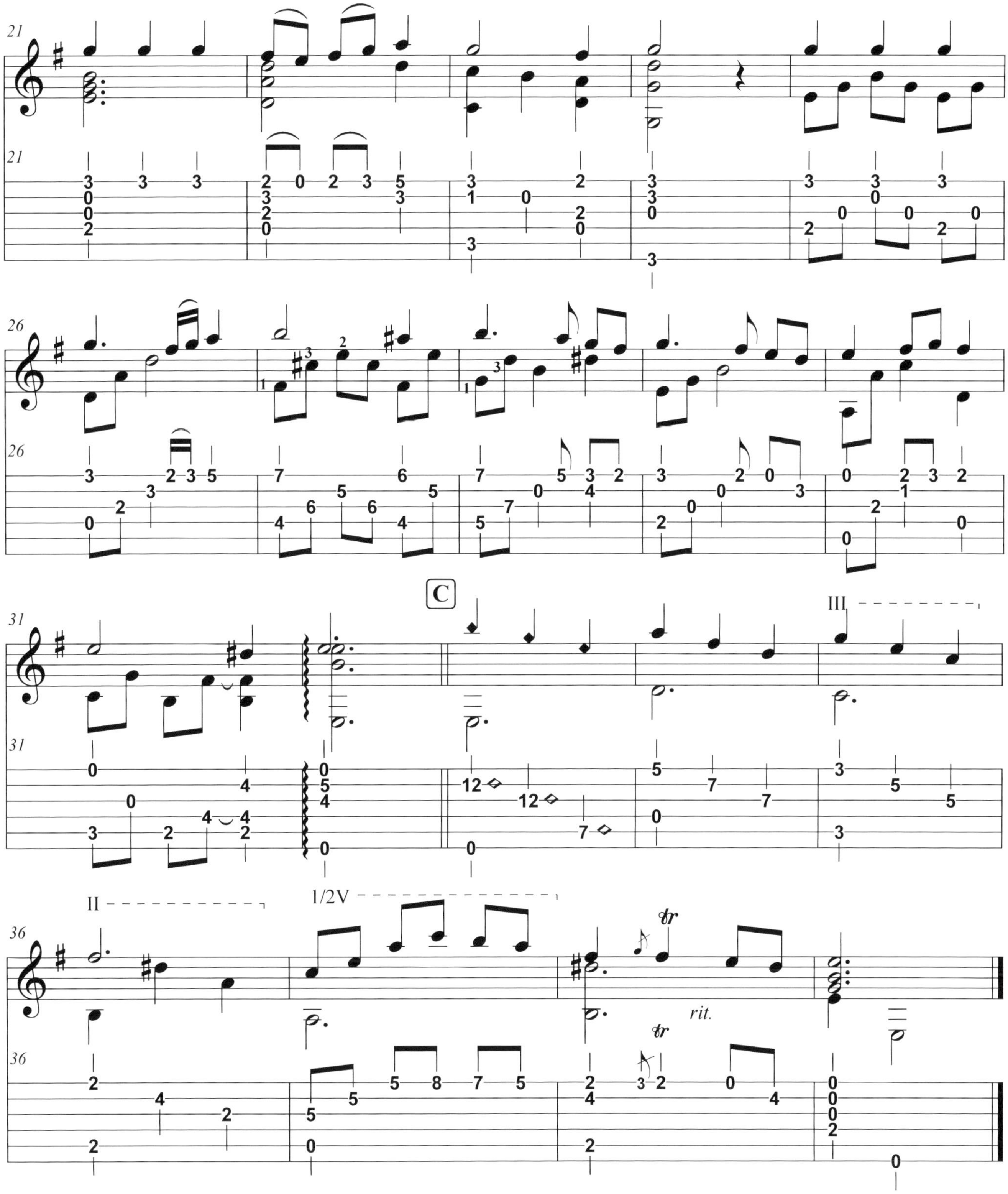
C
III
II
1/2V
rit.

13

Fortune My Foe

Moderato ♩ = 100

arr. Raymond Gonzalez

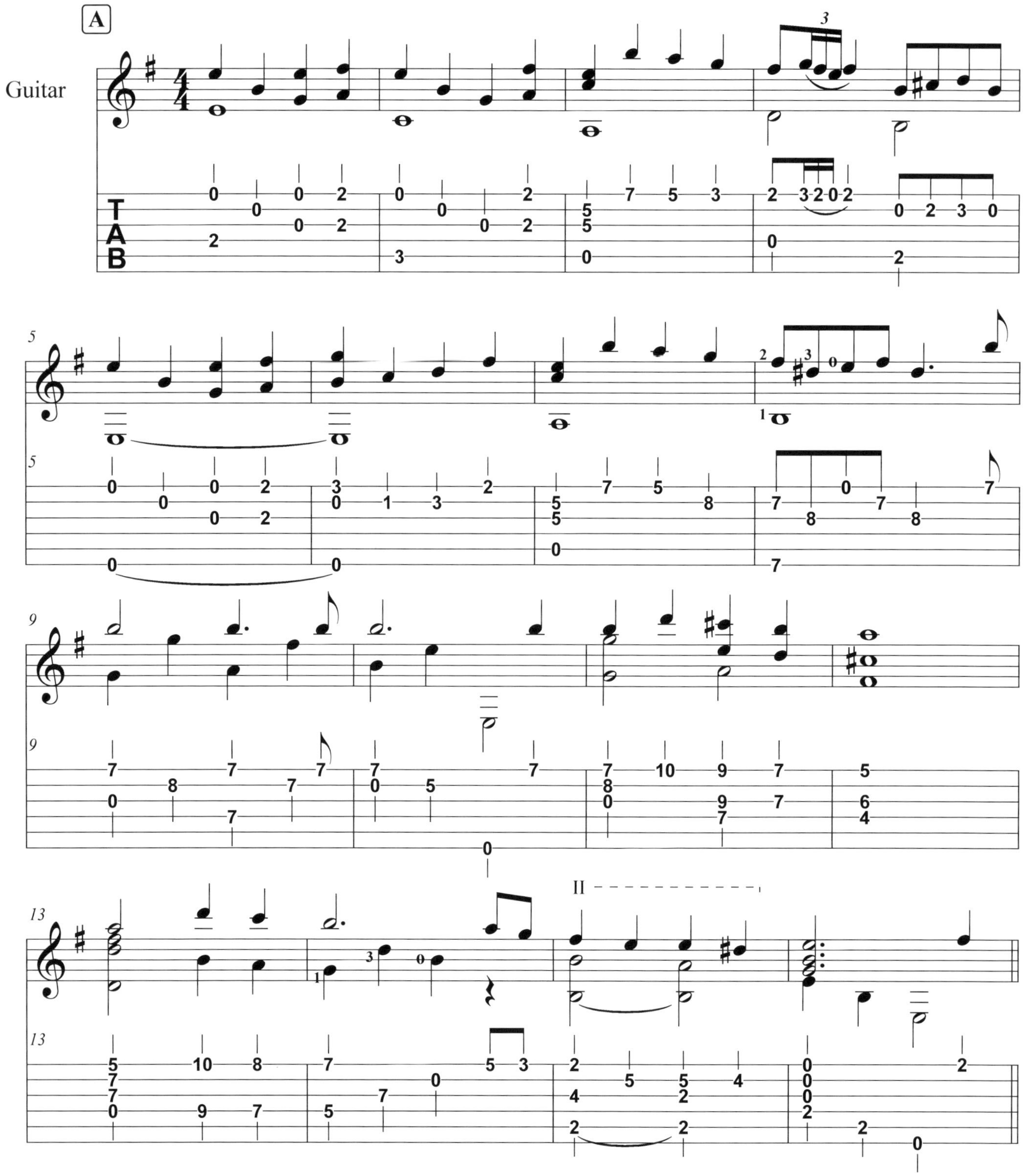

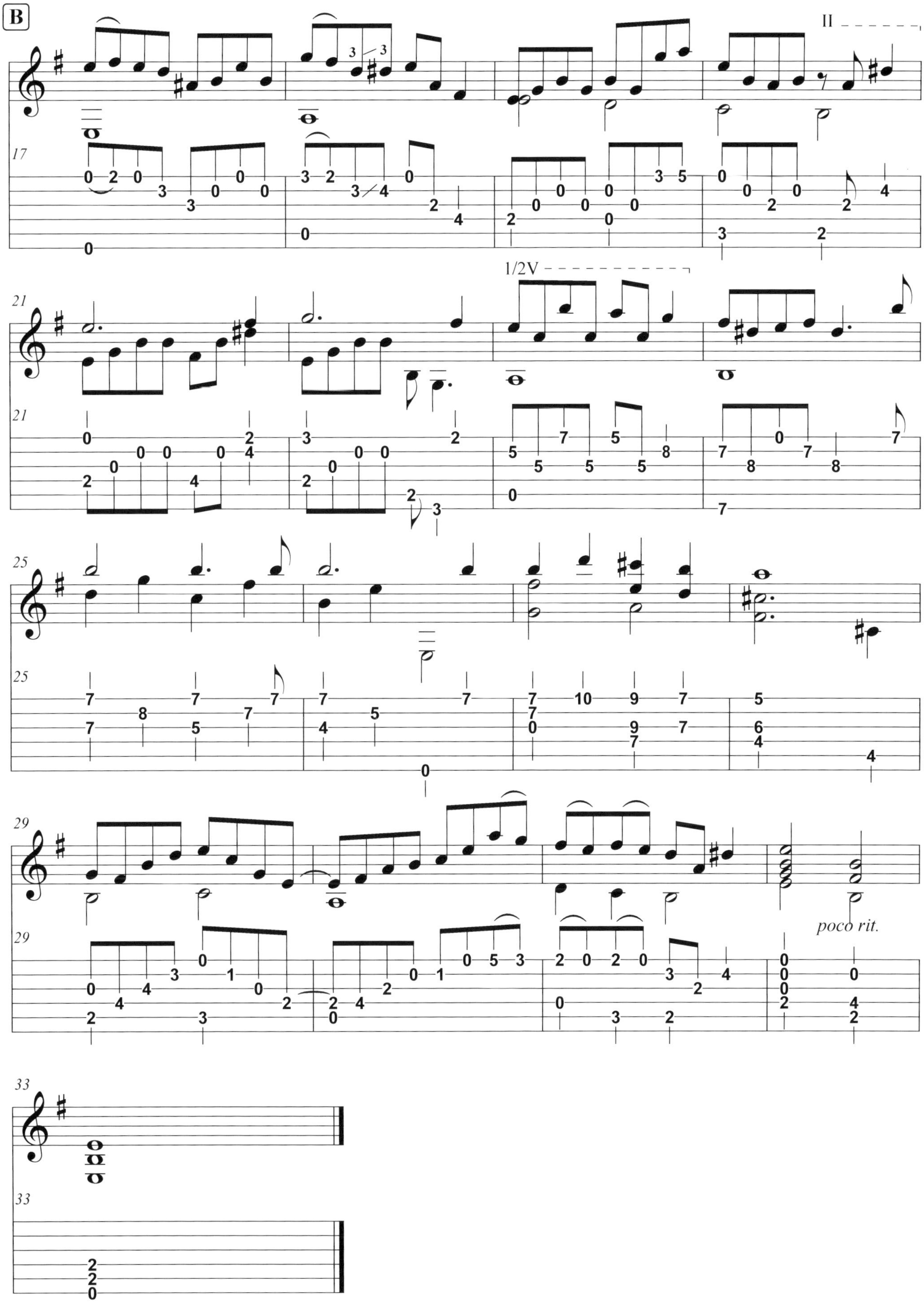
B
II
1/2V
poco rit.

Chestnut

John Playford
arr. Raymond Gonzalez

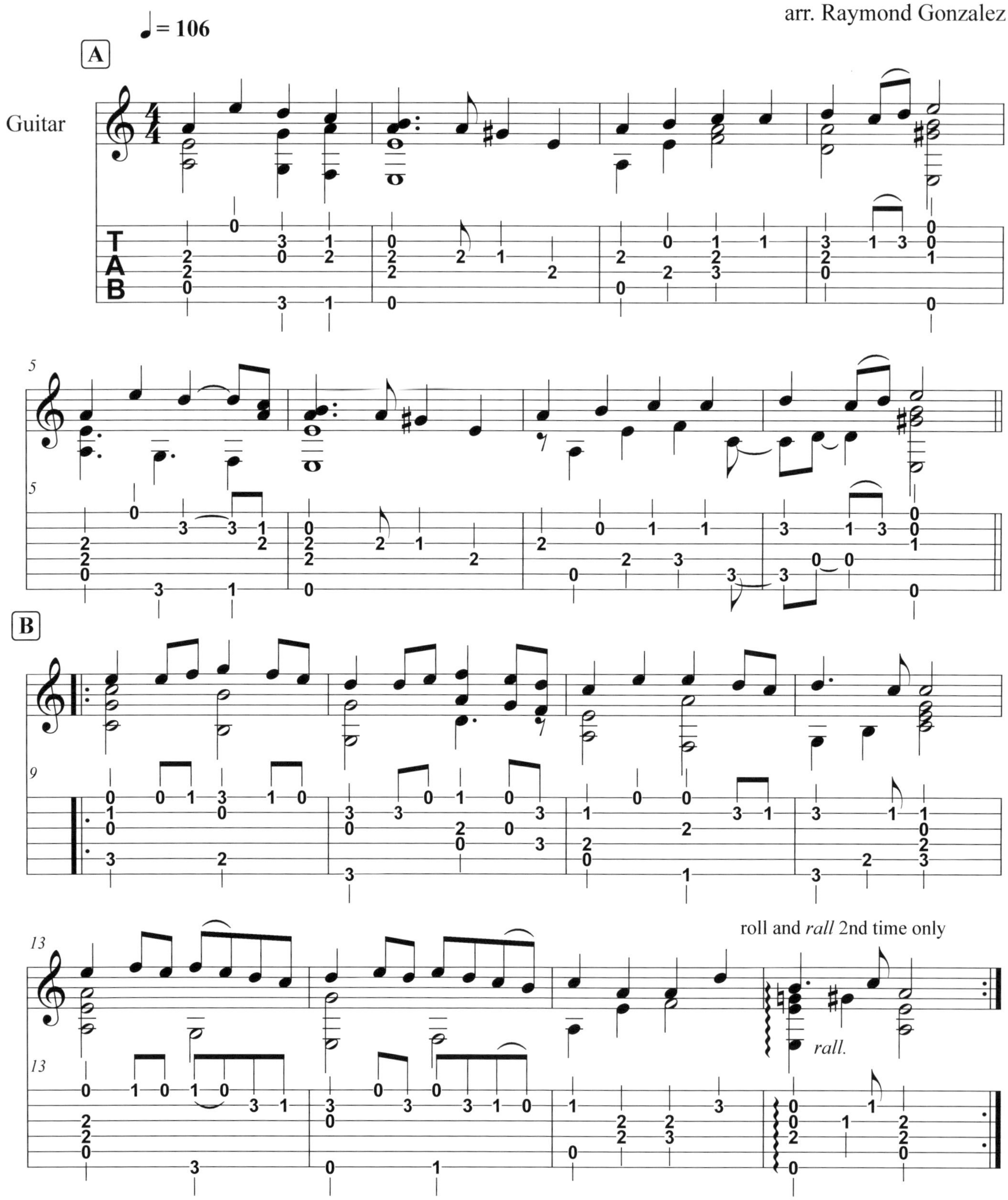

15

Gavotte

Michael Praetorius
arr. Raymond Gonzalez

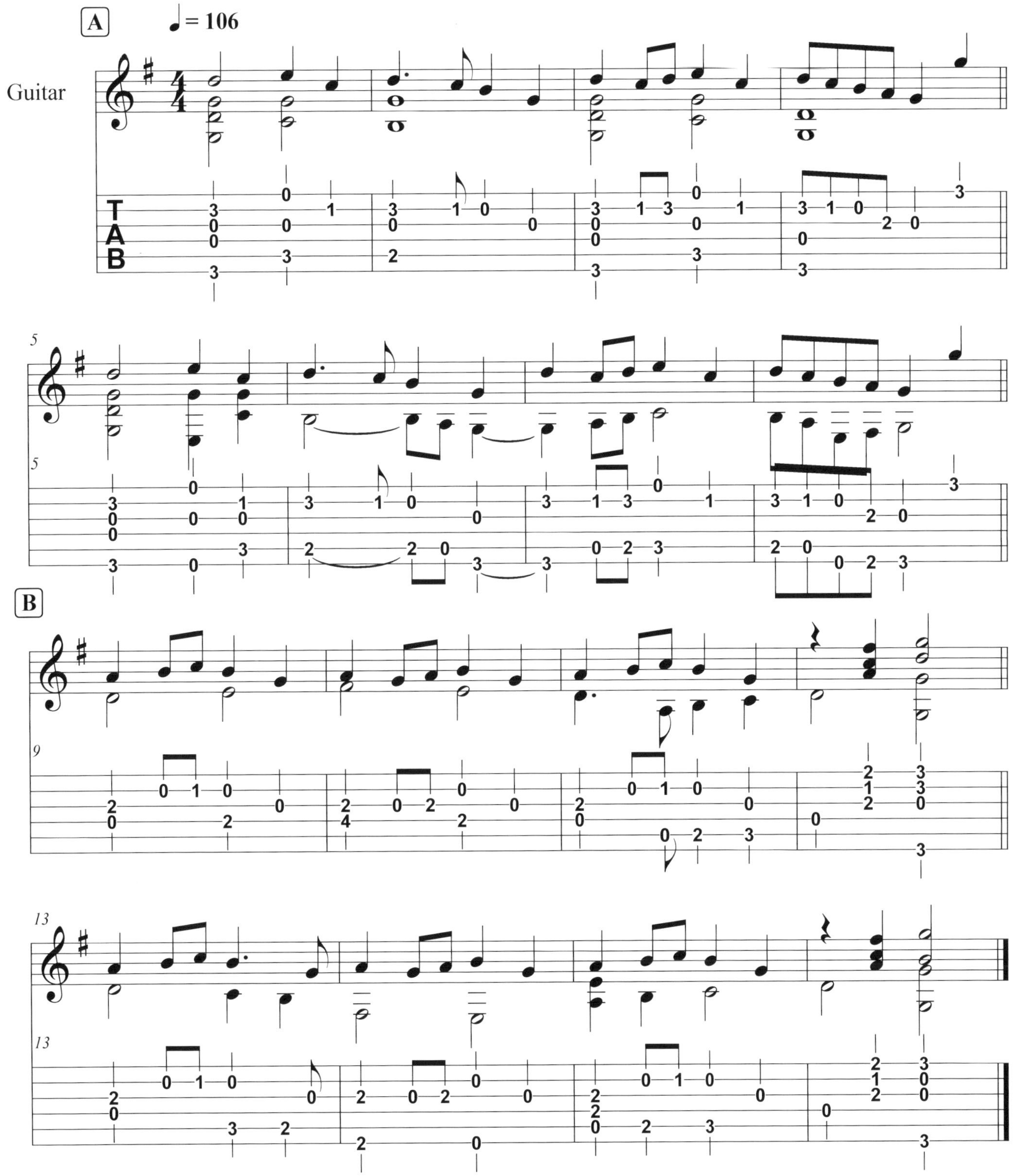

16

Greensleeves

⑥ = D

arr. Raymond Gonzalez

Andante

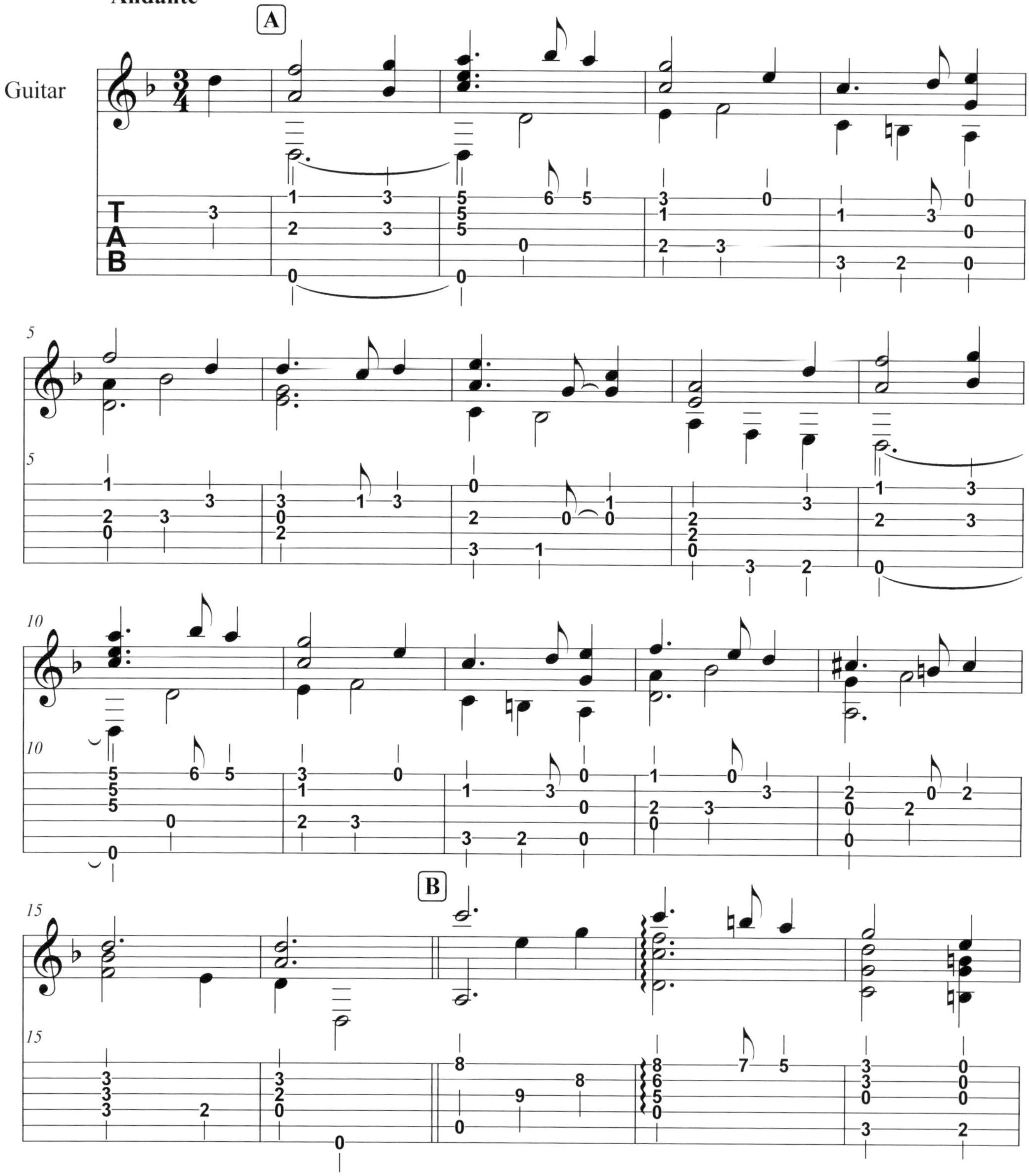

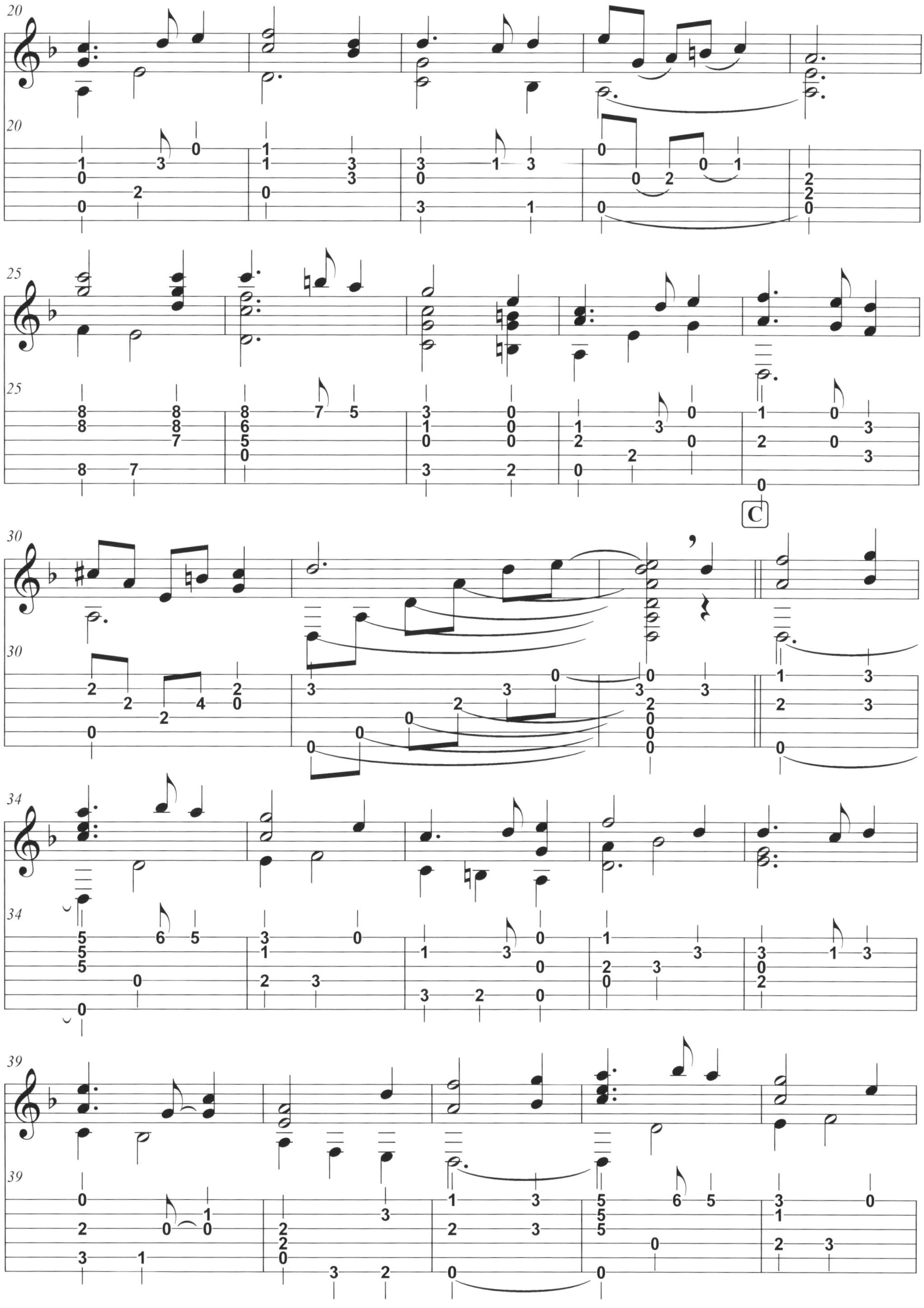
C

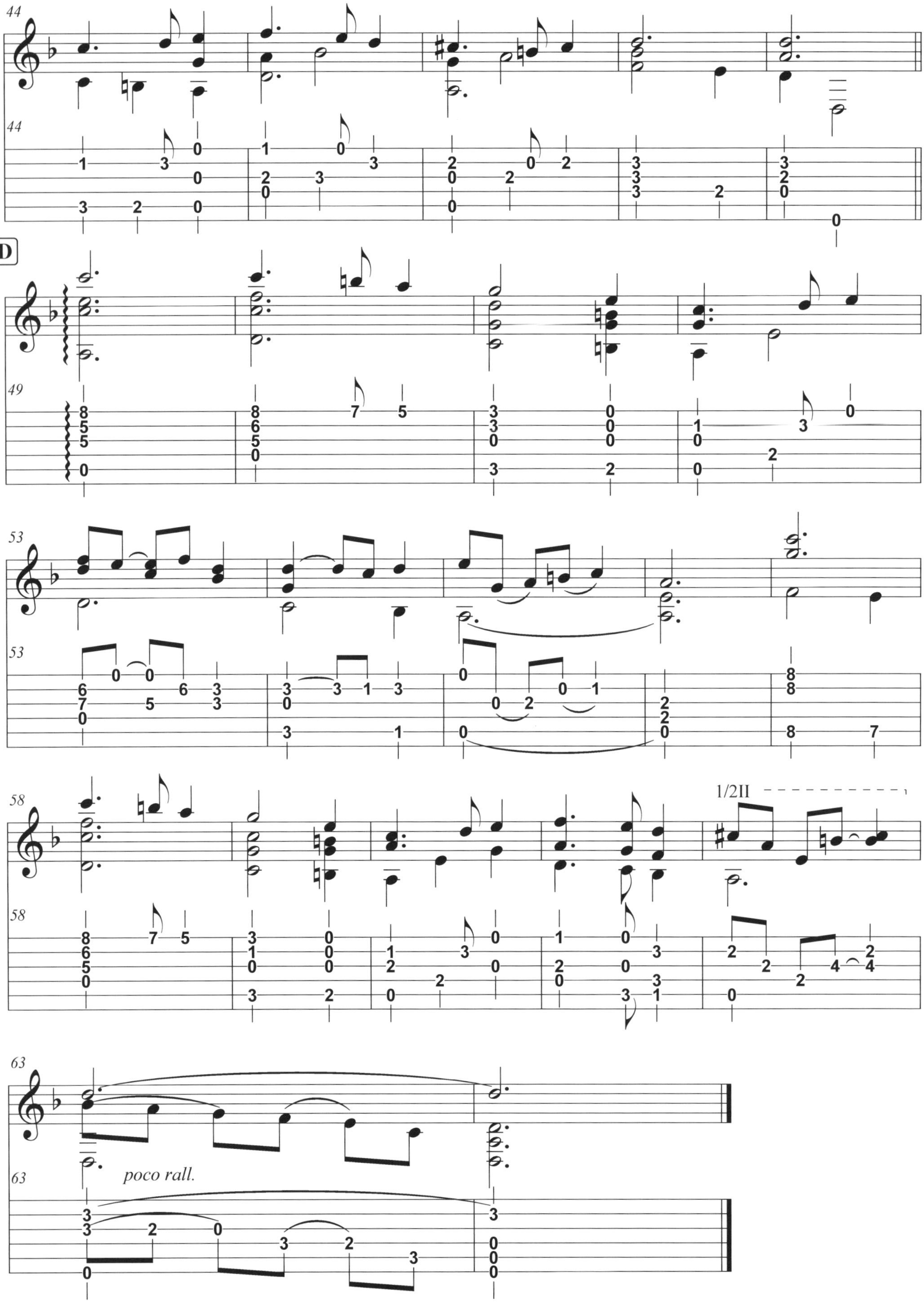
44
D
49
53
58
1/2II
63
poco rall.

17

Greensleeves
with key change

⑥ = D

arr. Raymond Gonzalez

Andante

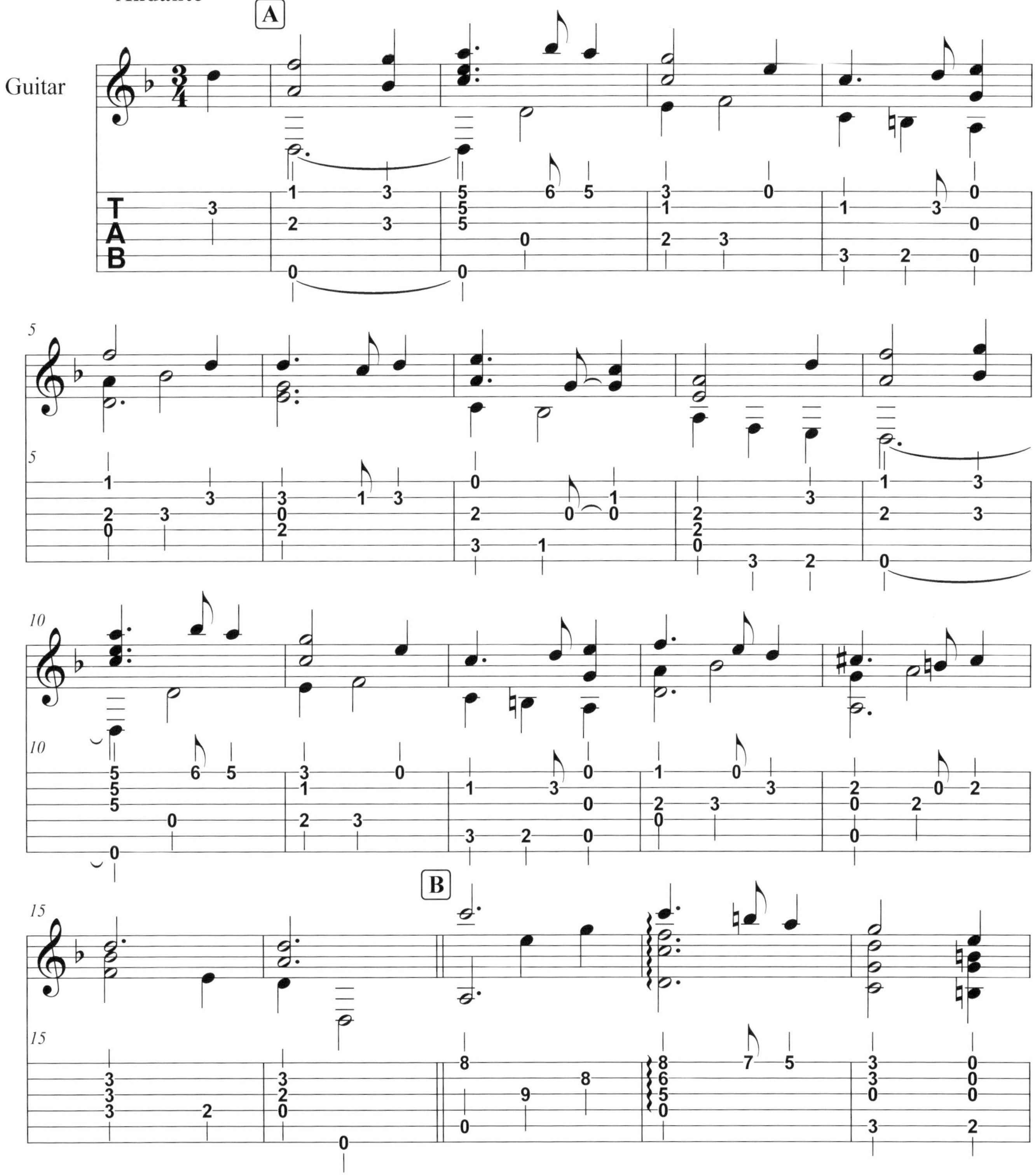

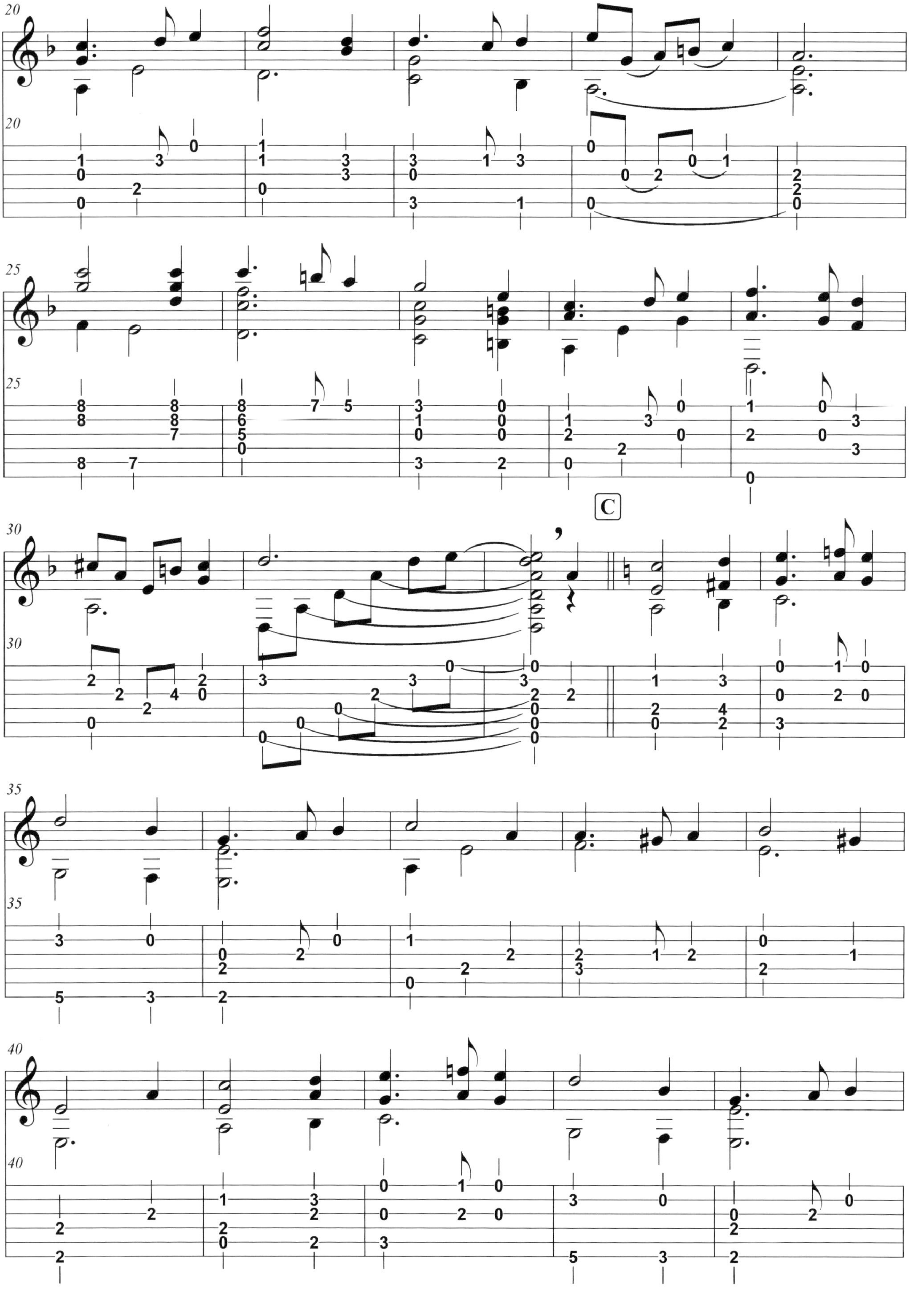
C

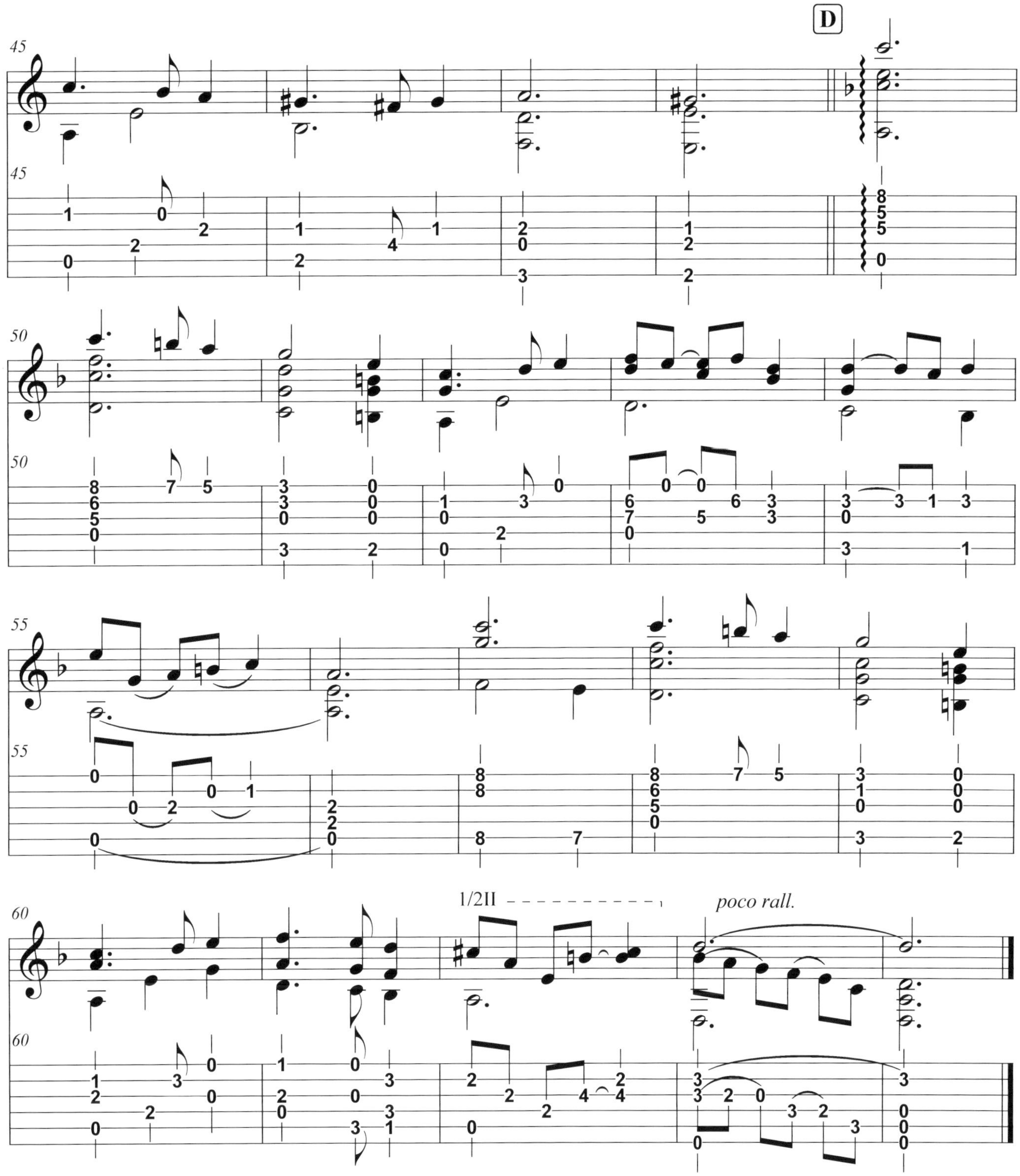
D
1/2II
poco rall.

18

Guardeme las vacas

Luis de Narváez
arr. Raymond Gonzalez

Allegro ♩ = 120

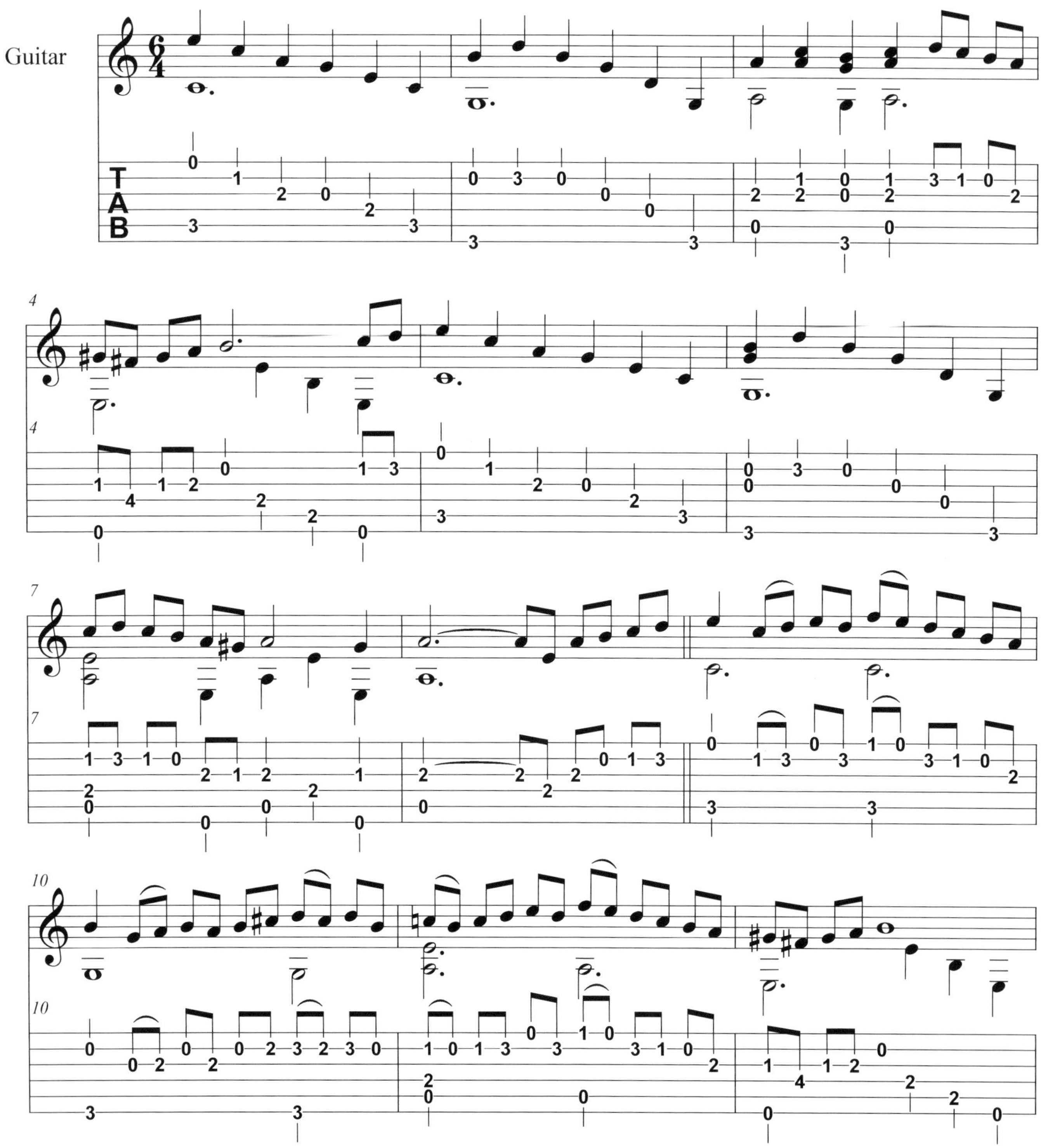

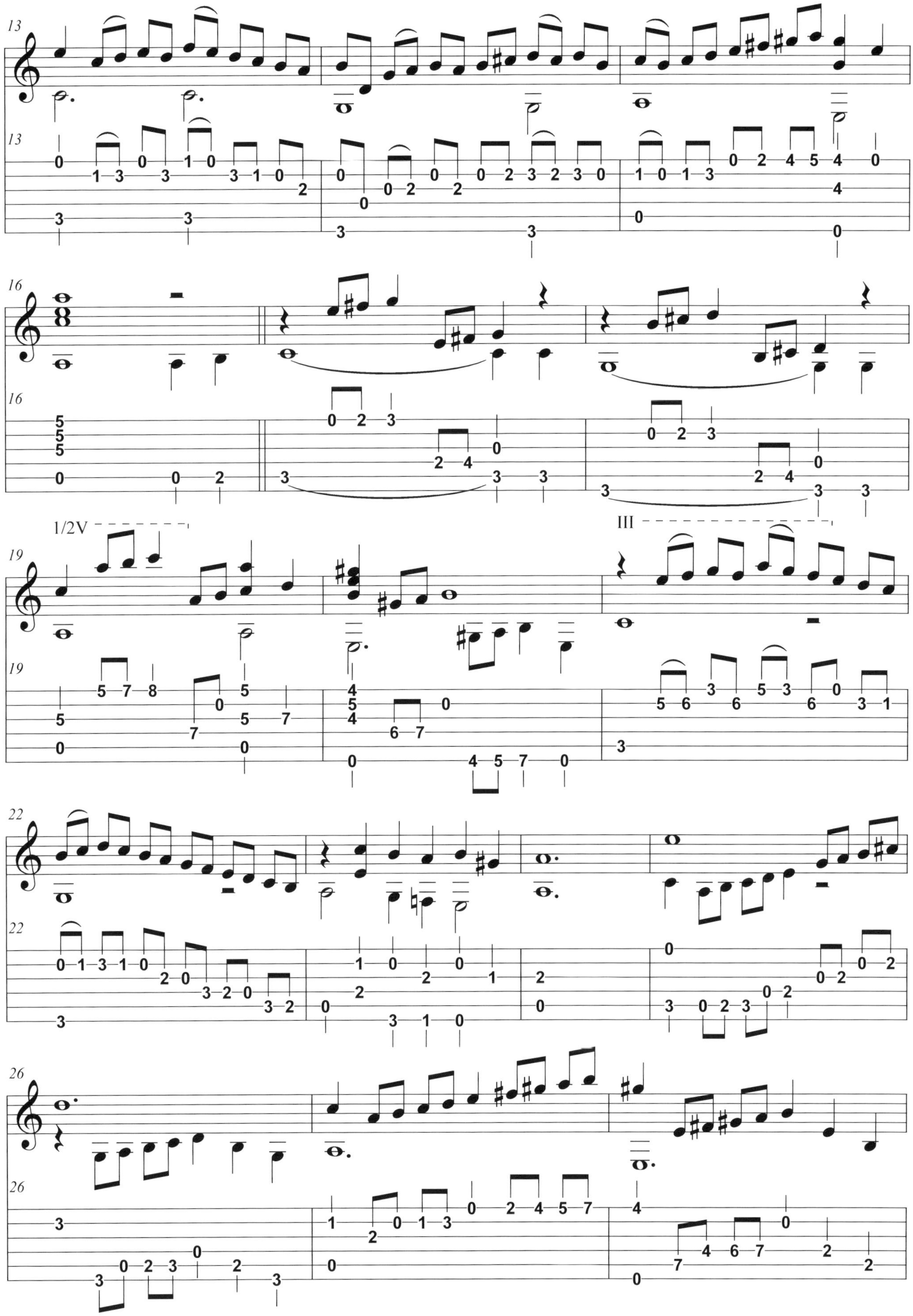
1/2V
III

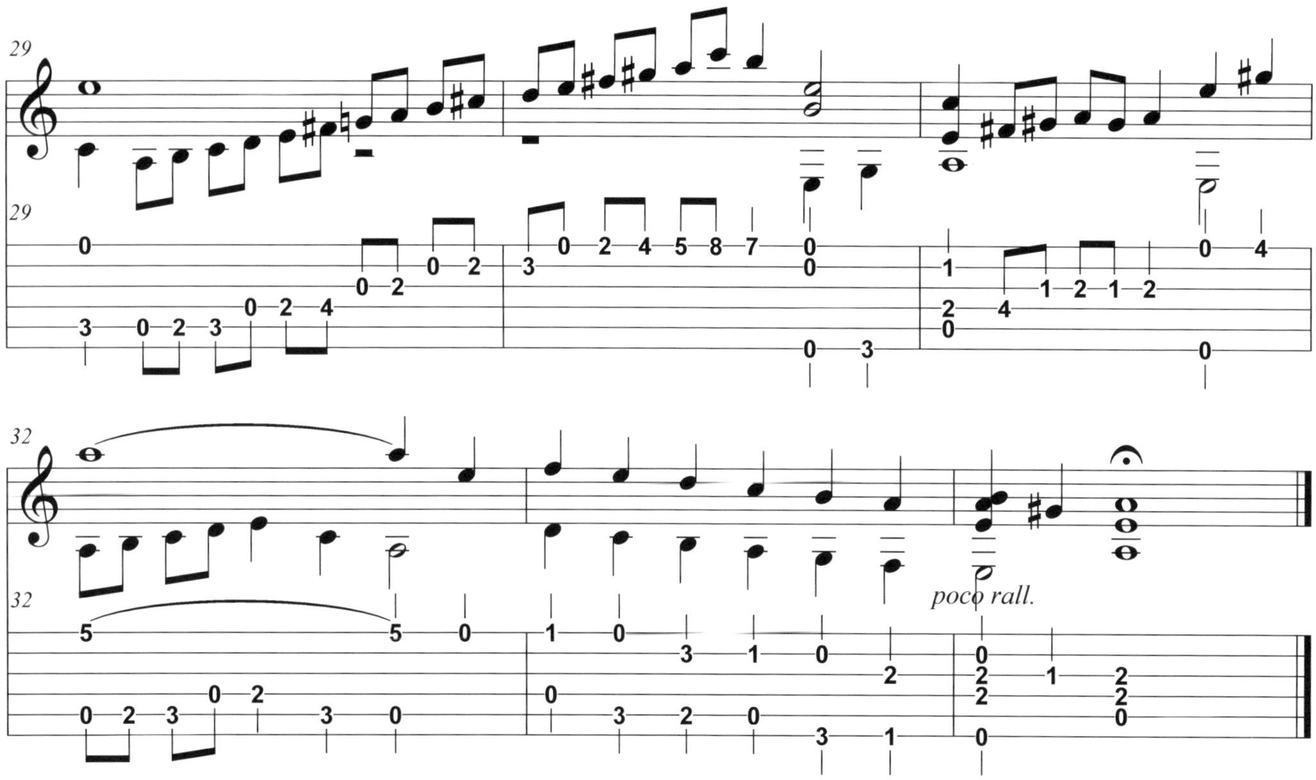

poco rall.

This page has been left blank to avoid an awward page turn.

19

Grimstock

arr. Raymond Gonzalez

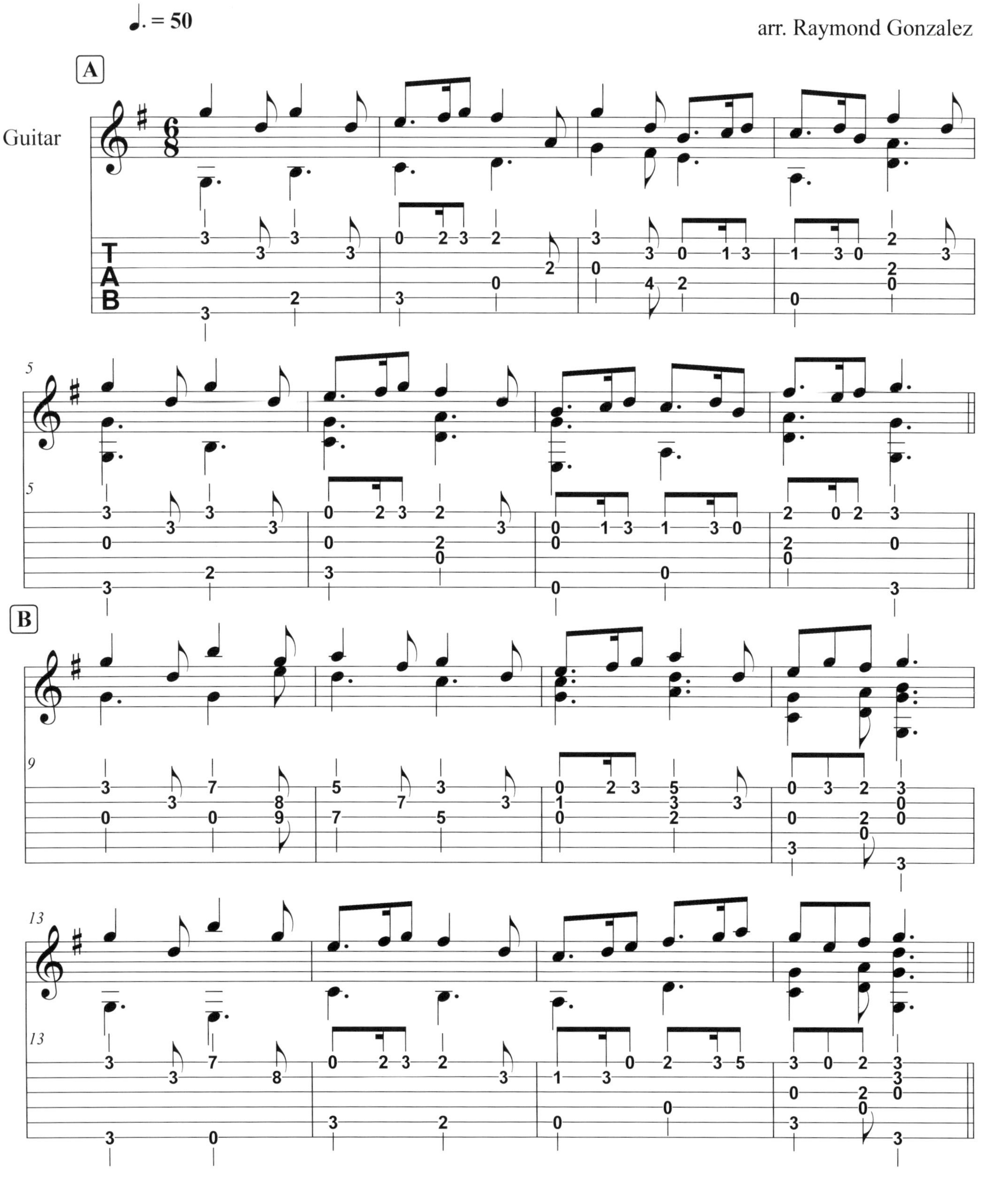

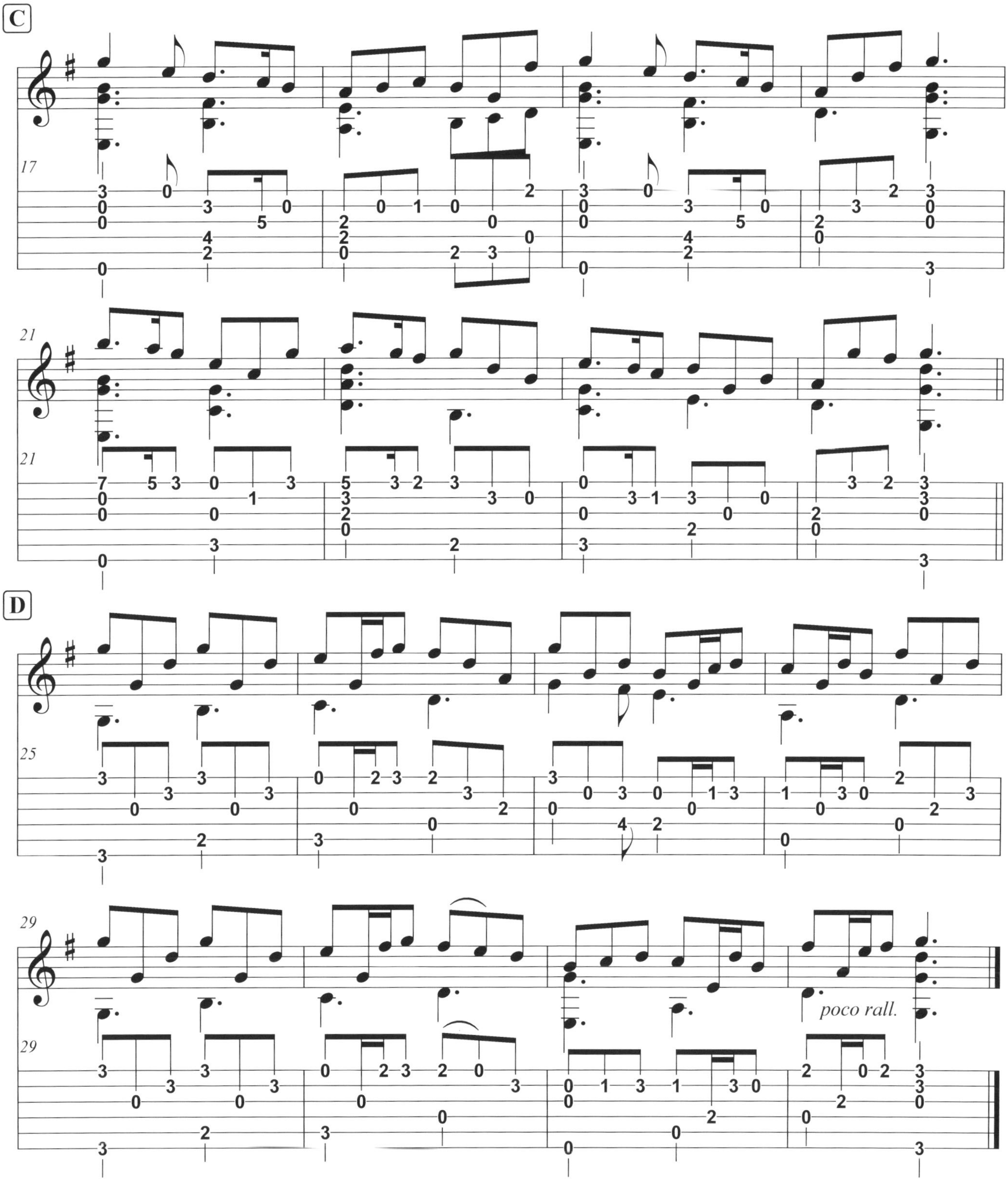
C
D
poco rall.

20

Kemp's Jig

♩= 110

arr. Raymond Gonzalez

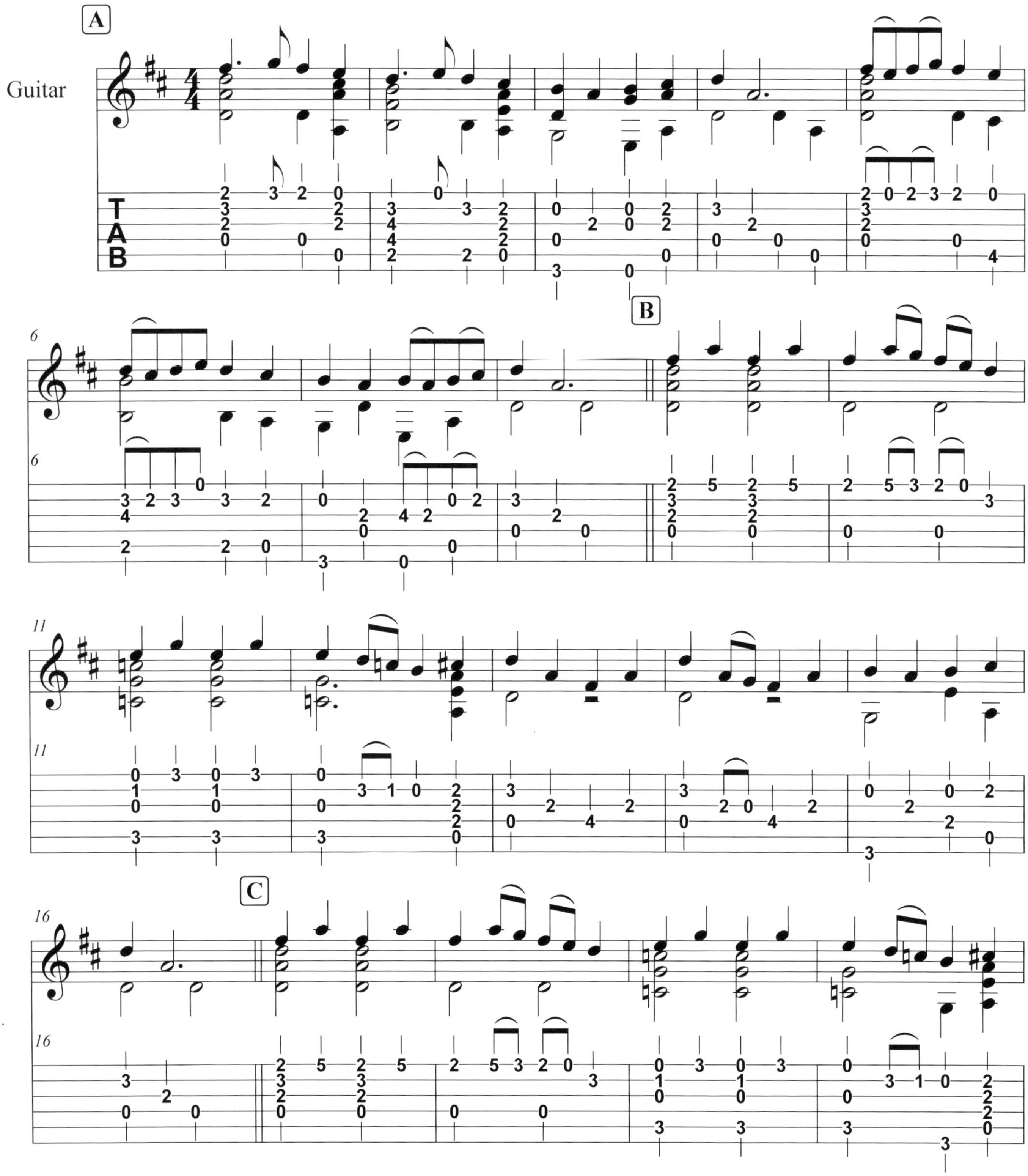

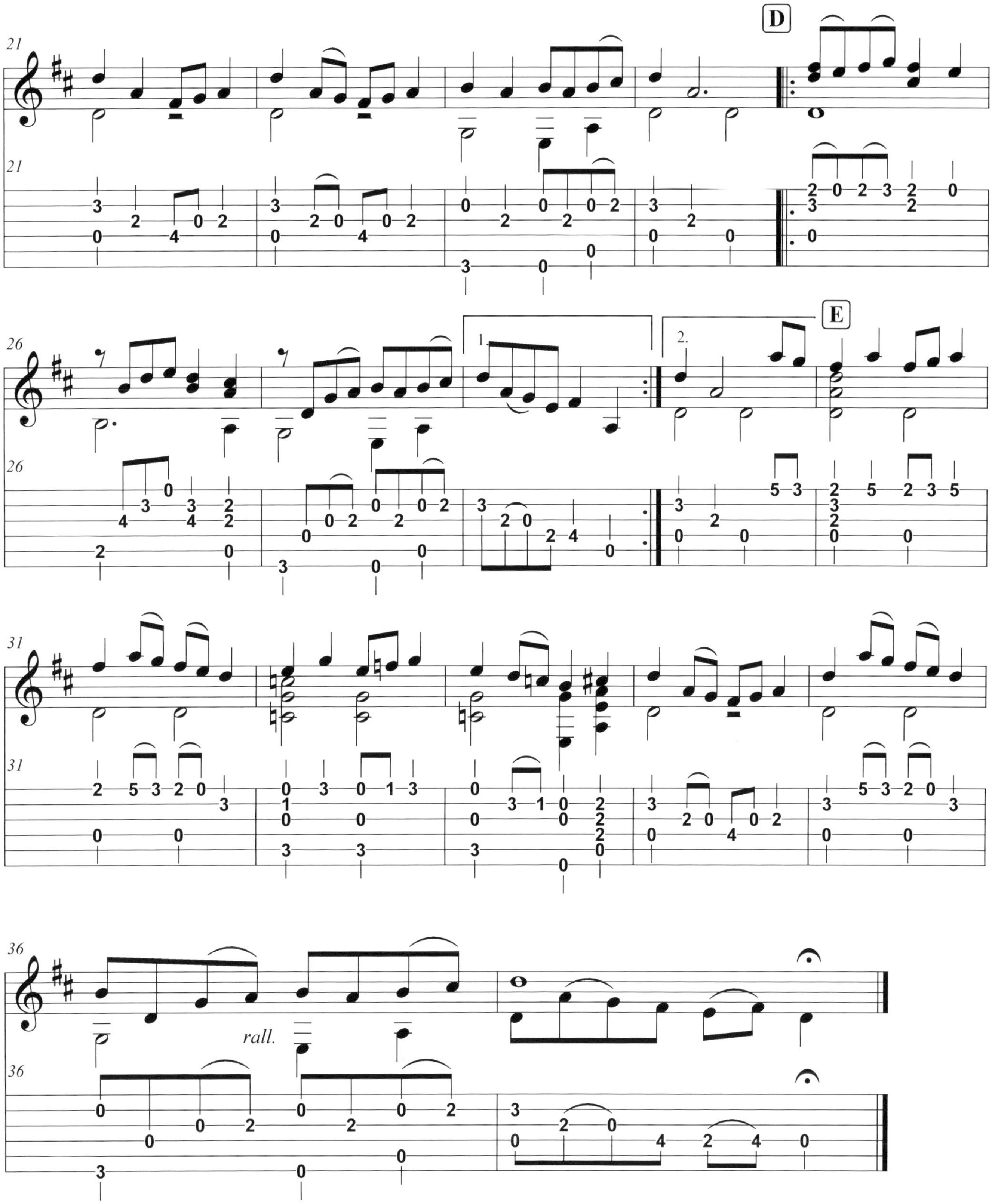
D
E
1.
2.
rall.

21

La Folias

⑥ = D

arr. Raymond Gonzalez

♩ = 118 Freely

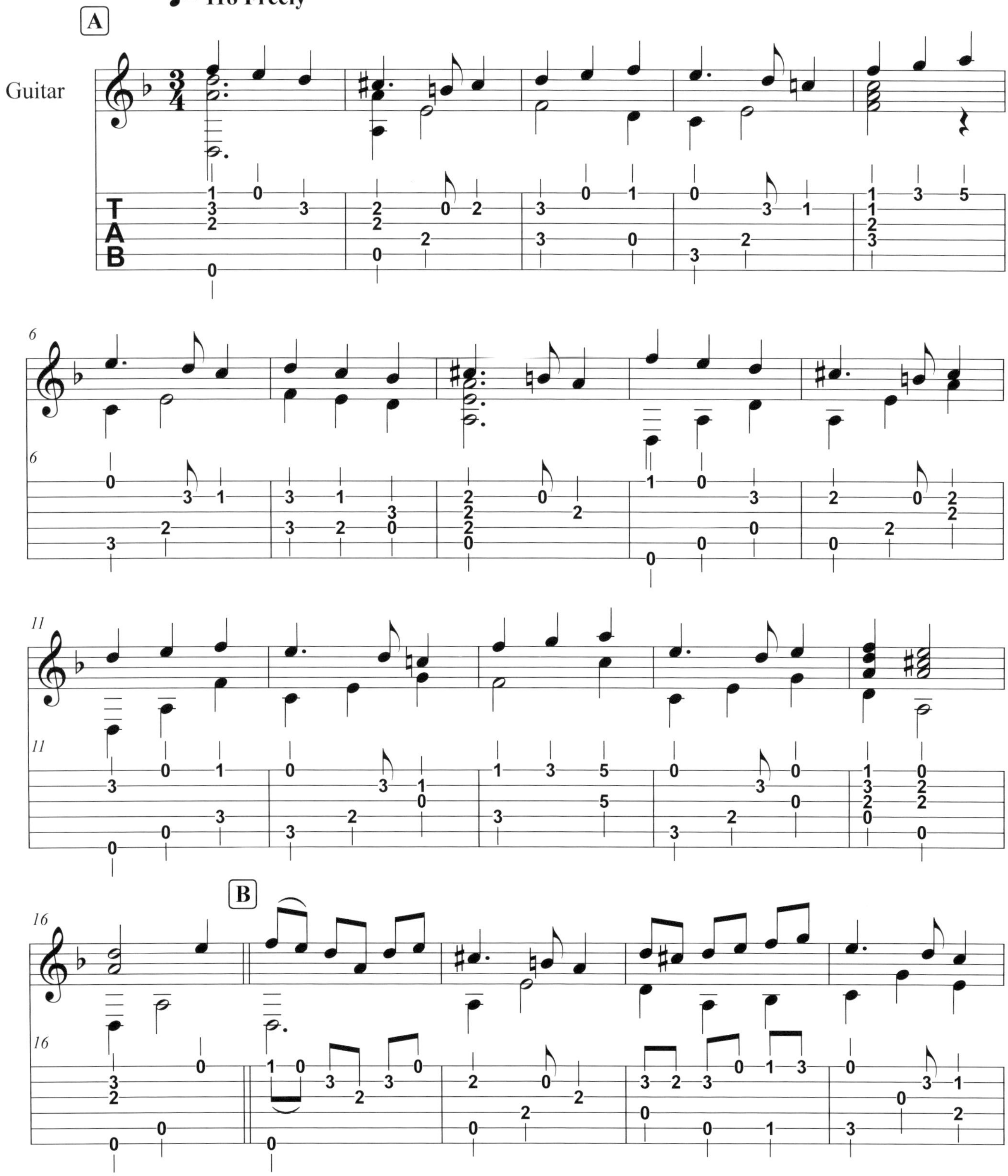

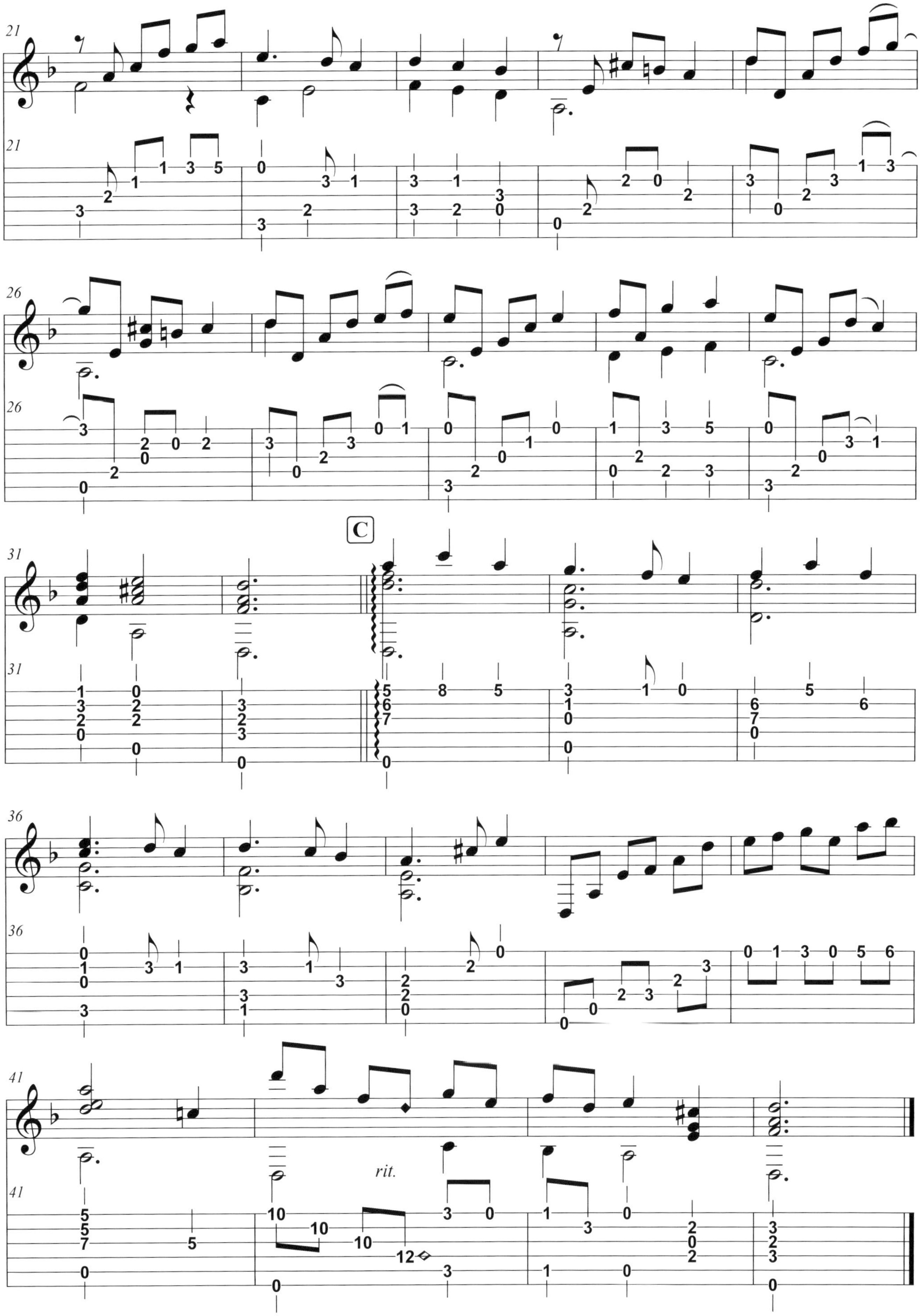
21
21
26
26
C
31
31
36
36
41
rit.
41

22

Moderato

⑥ = D

Moderato ♩ = 76

Anonymous
arr. Raymond Gonzalez

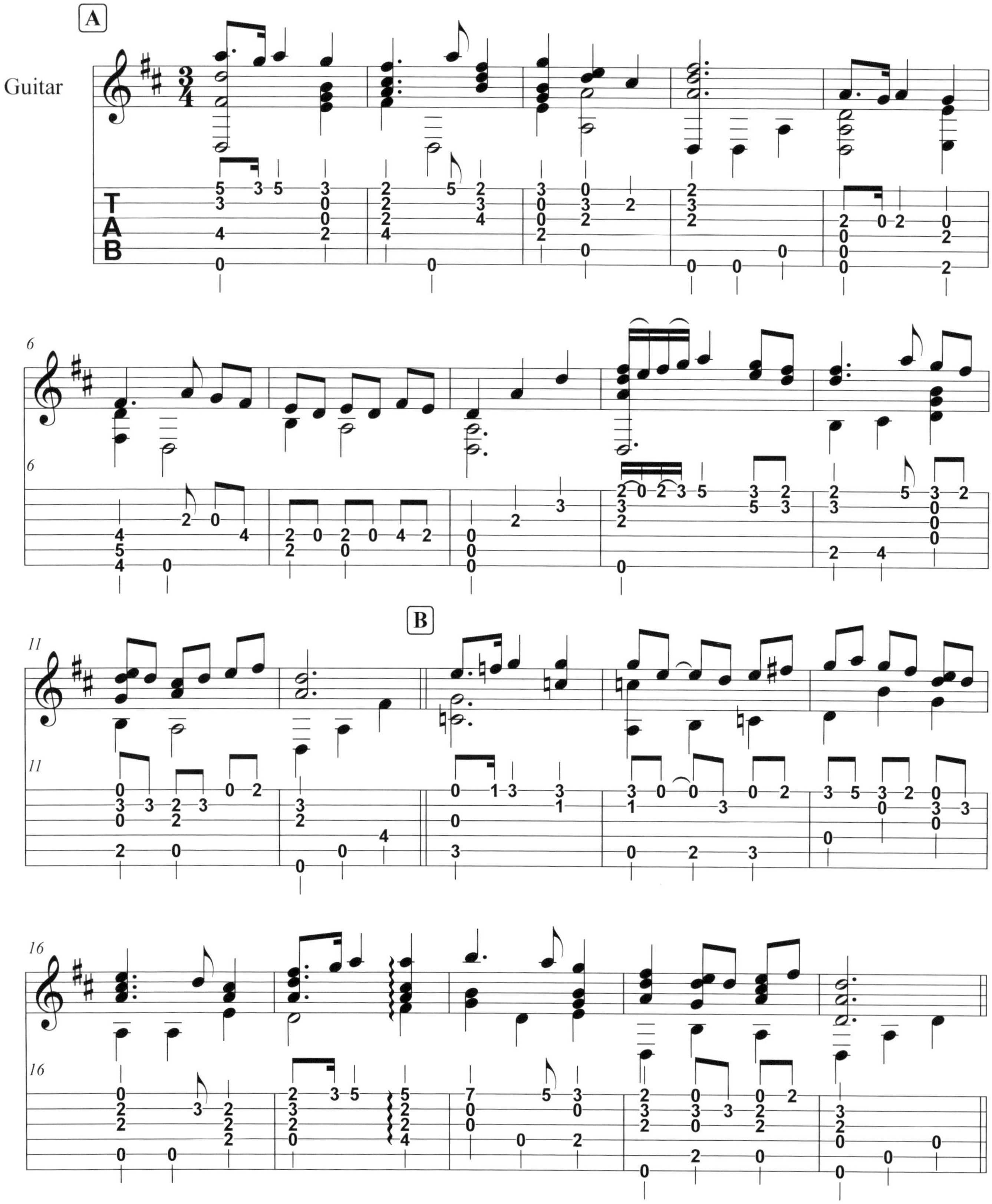

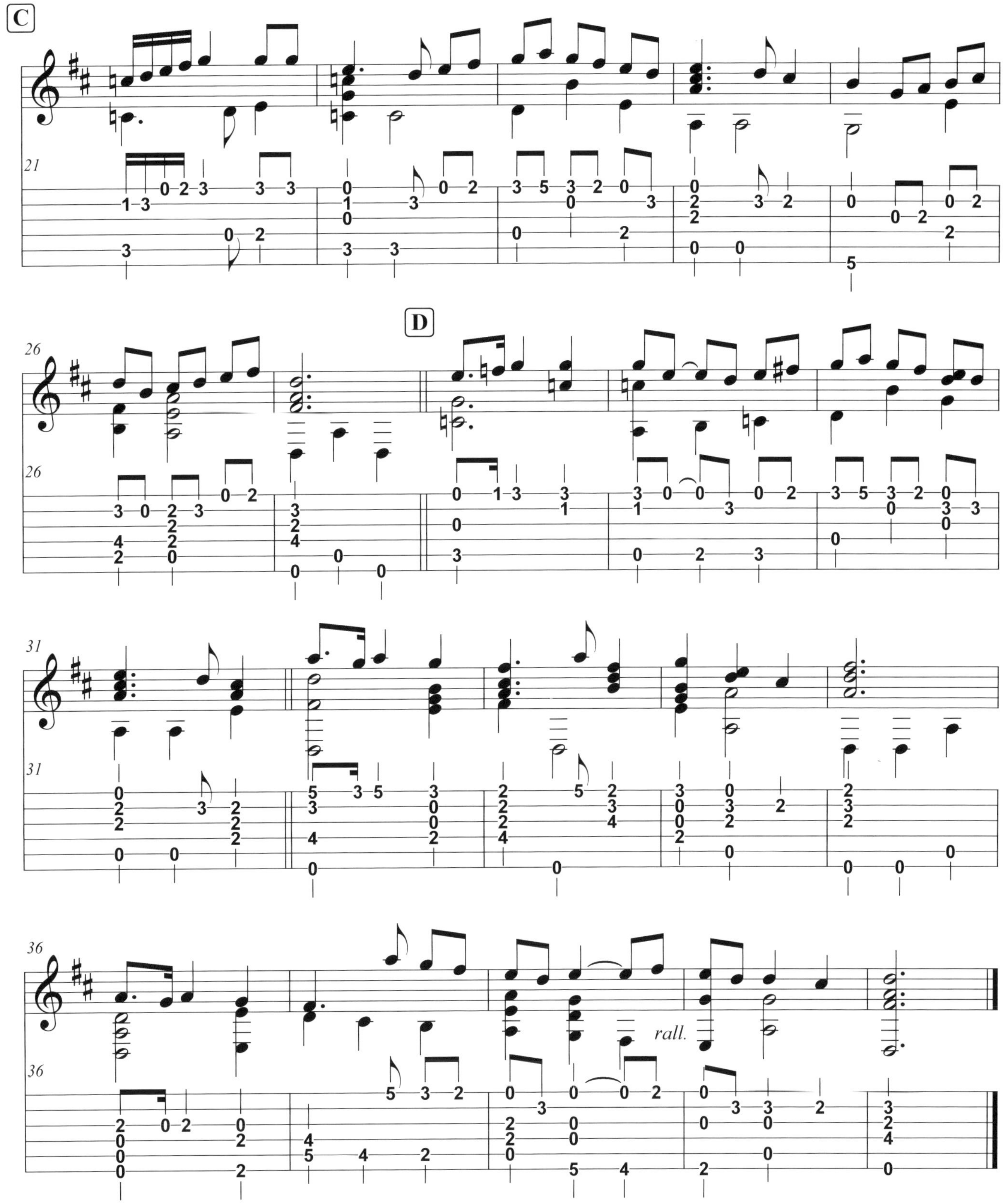
C
21
26
D
31
36
rall.

23

O Esca Viatorum

Louis Bourgeois 1549
arr. Raymond Gonzalez

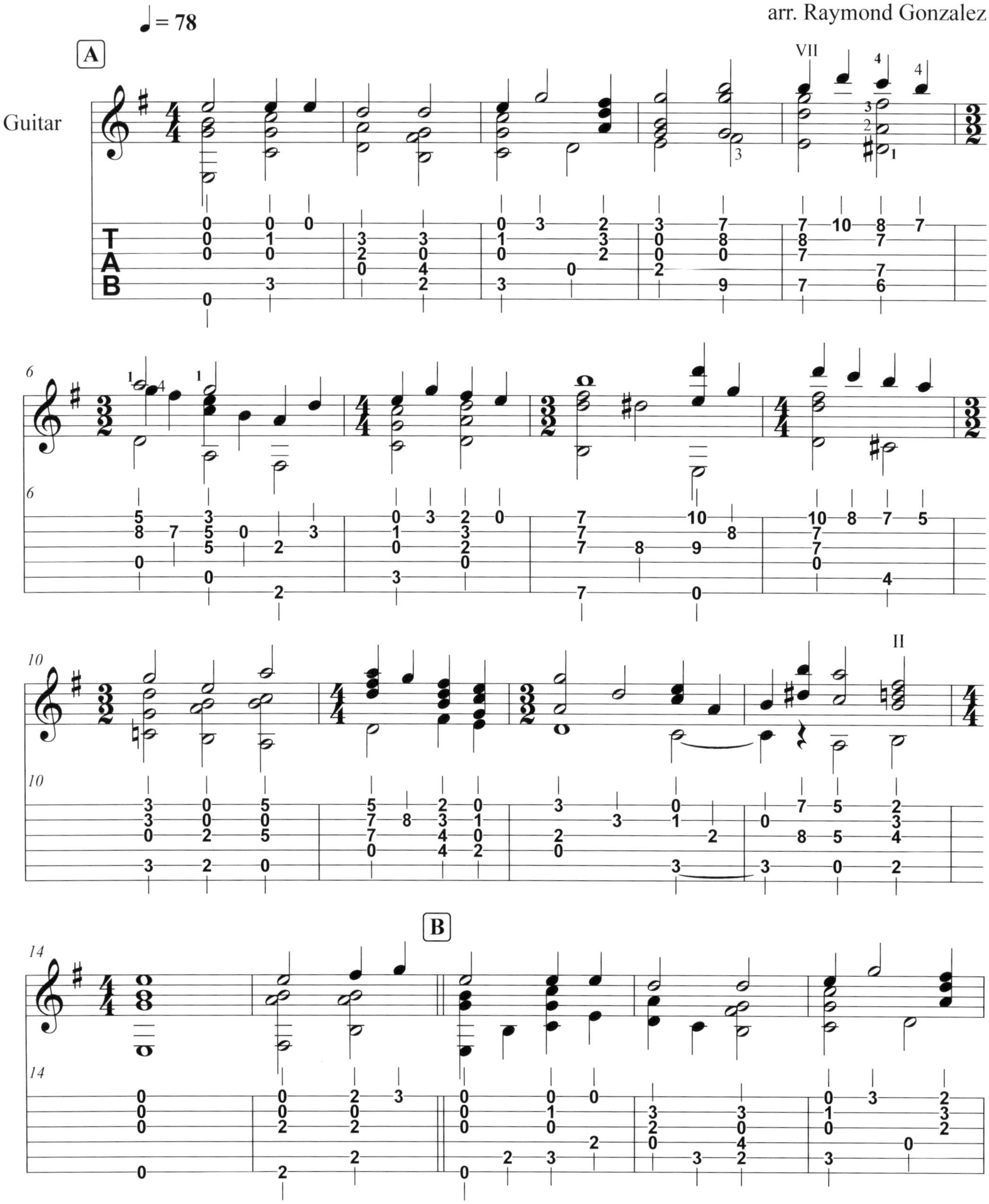

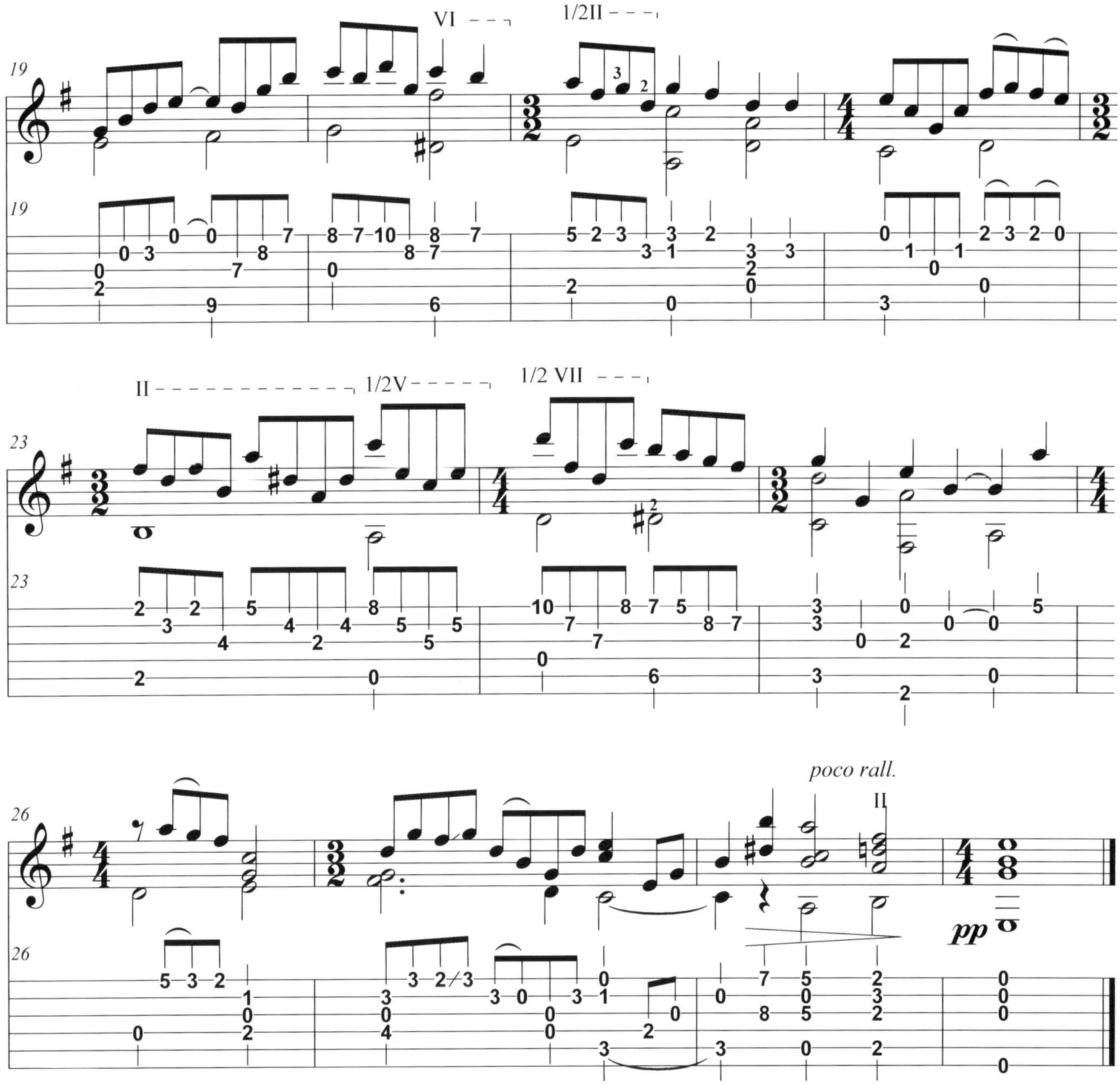
VI
1/2II
II
1/2V
1/2 VII
poco rall.
II
pp

24

Packington's Pound

♩= 110

arr. Raymond Gonzalez

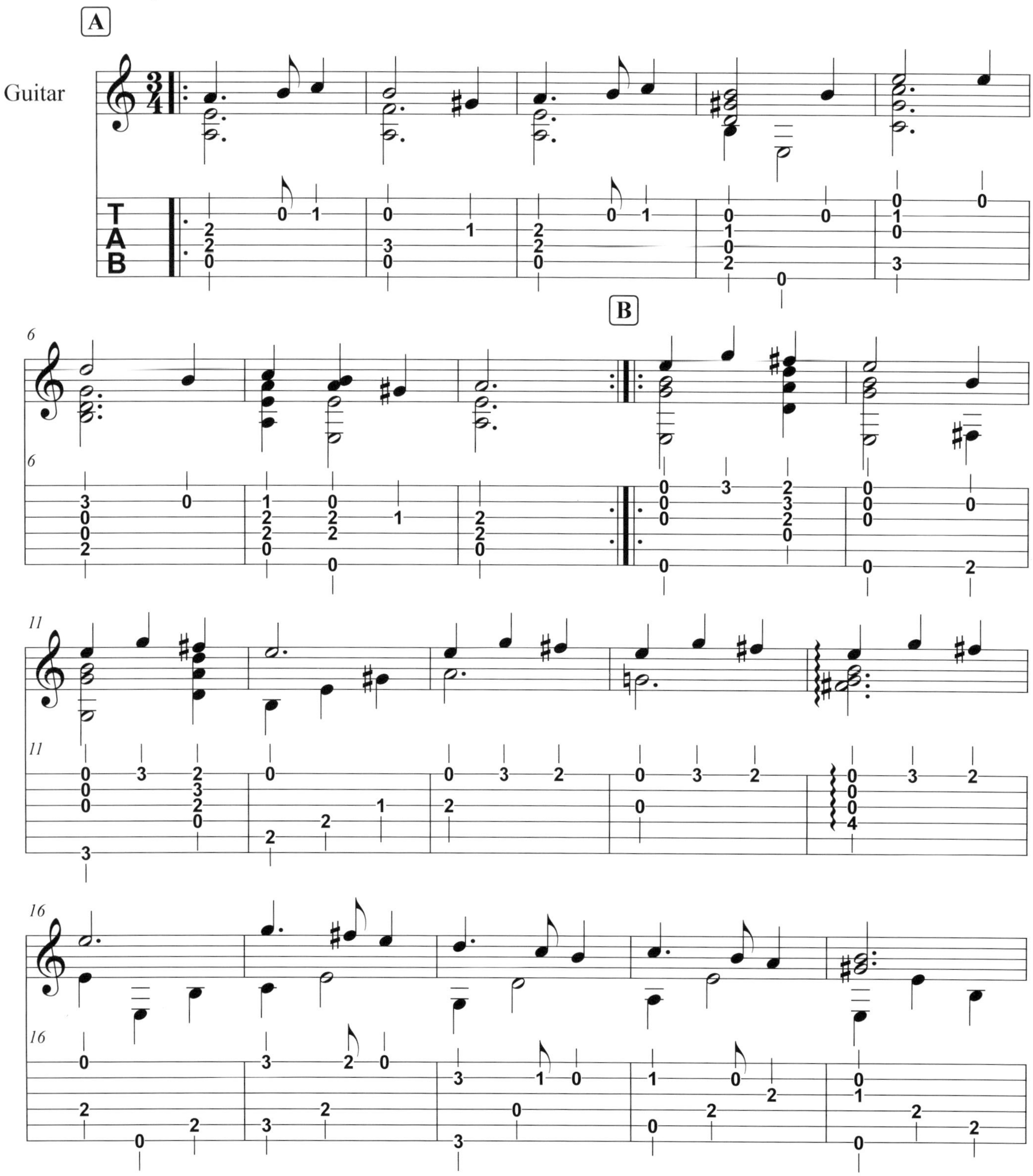

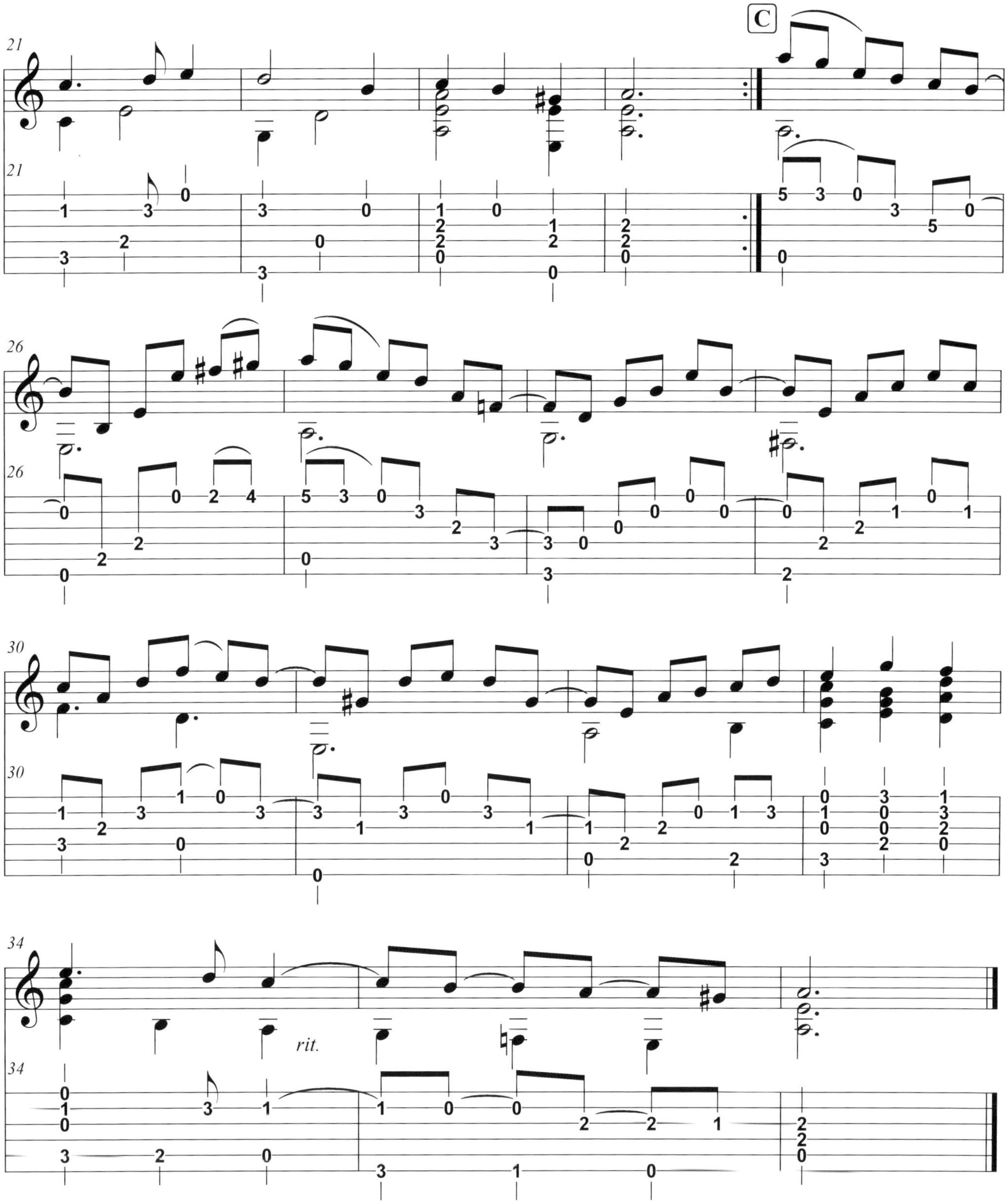
C
rit.

25

Pastourelle

13th Century French
arr. Raymond Gonzalez

♩ = 146

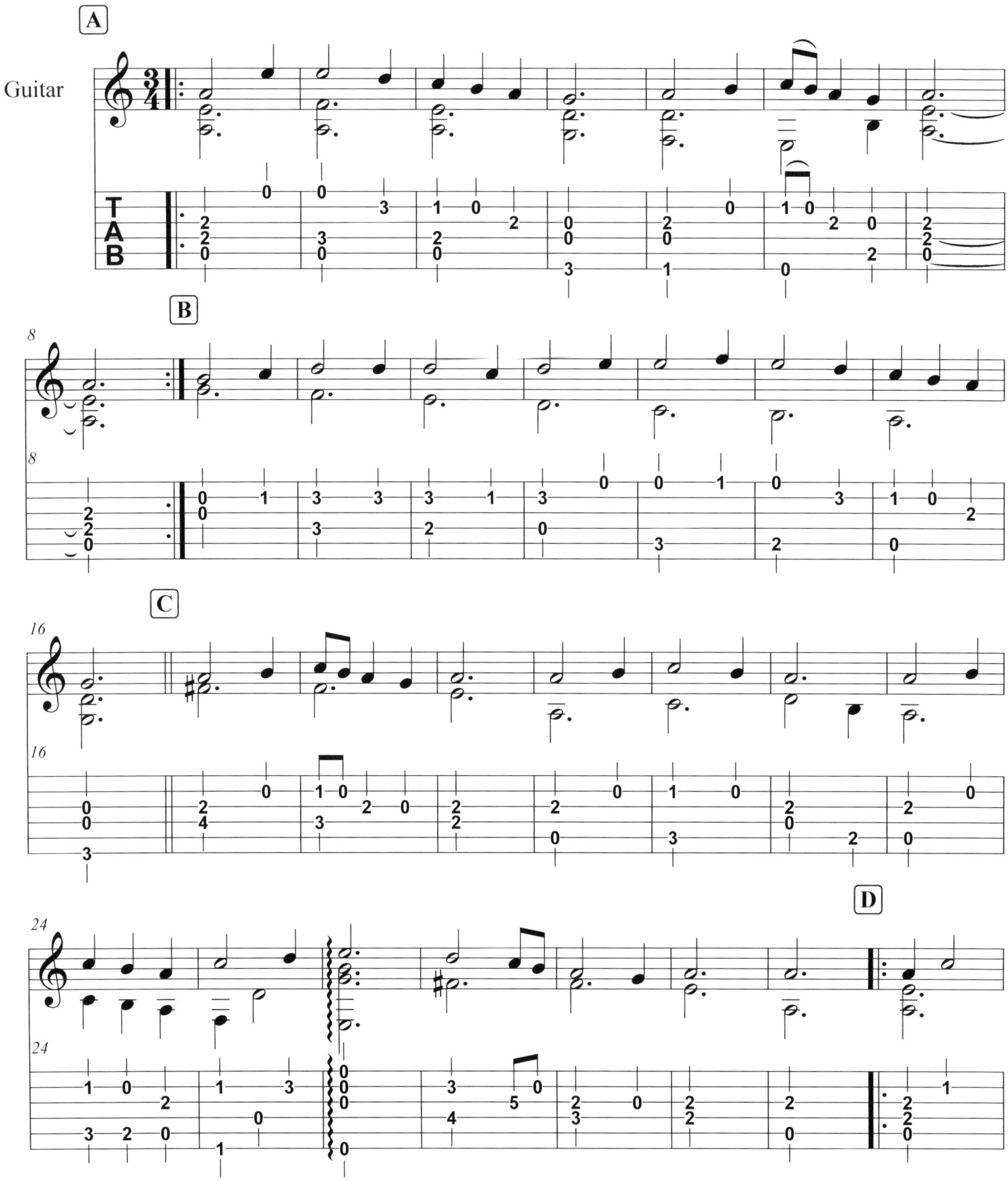

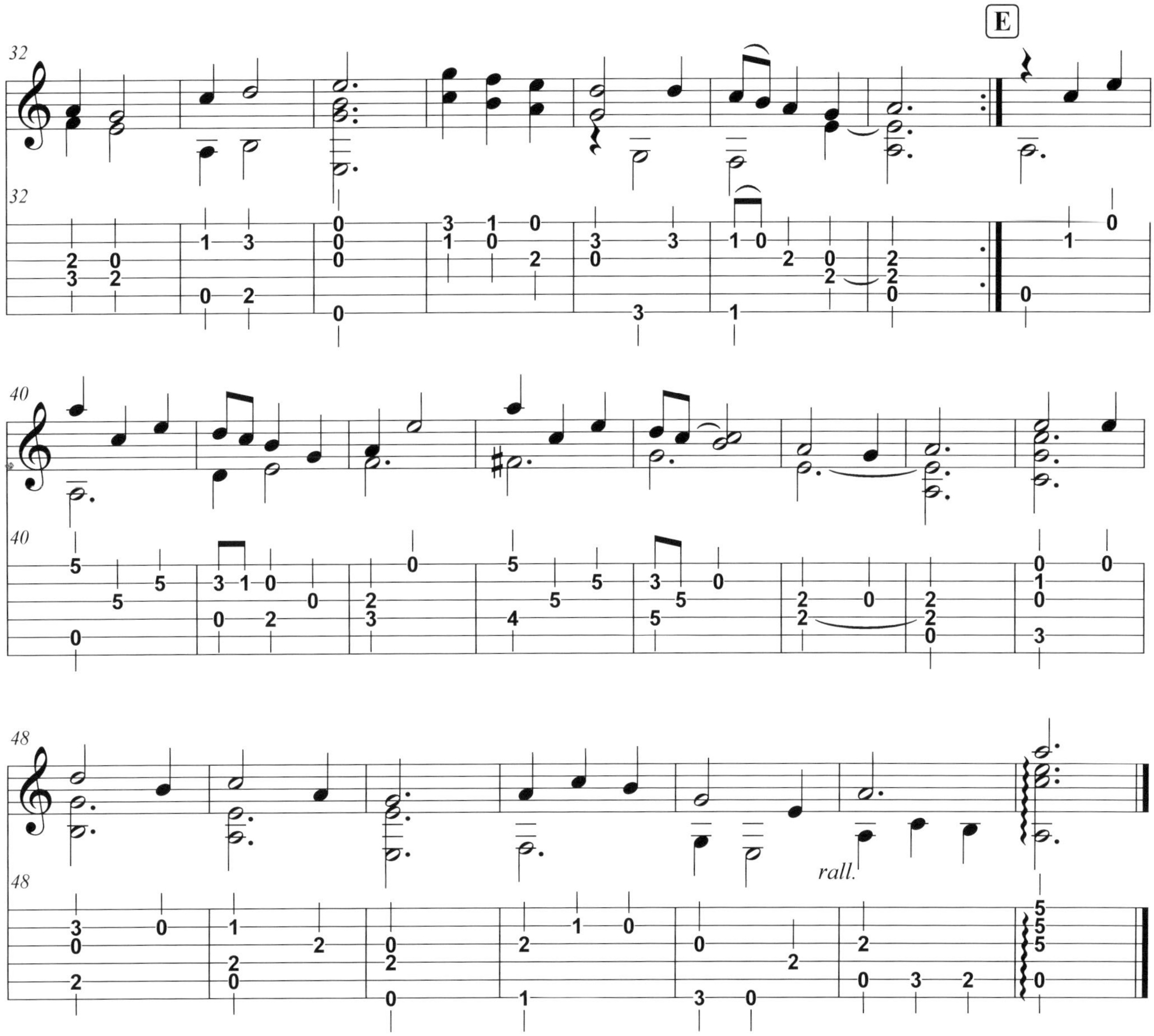
E
32
40
48
rall.

26

Rendez À Dieu

Louis Bourgeois 1543
arr. Raymond Gonzalez

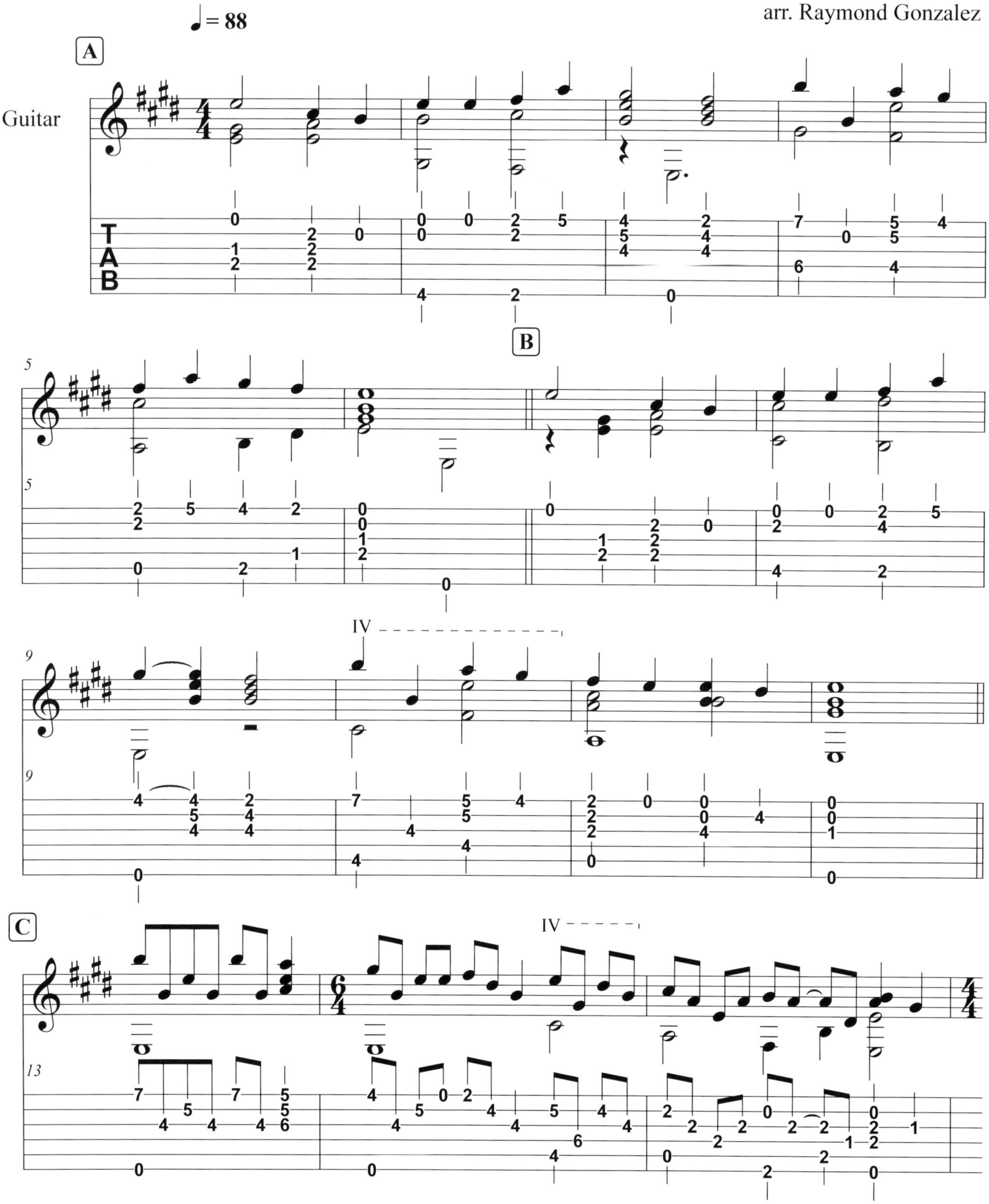

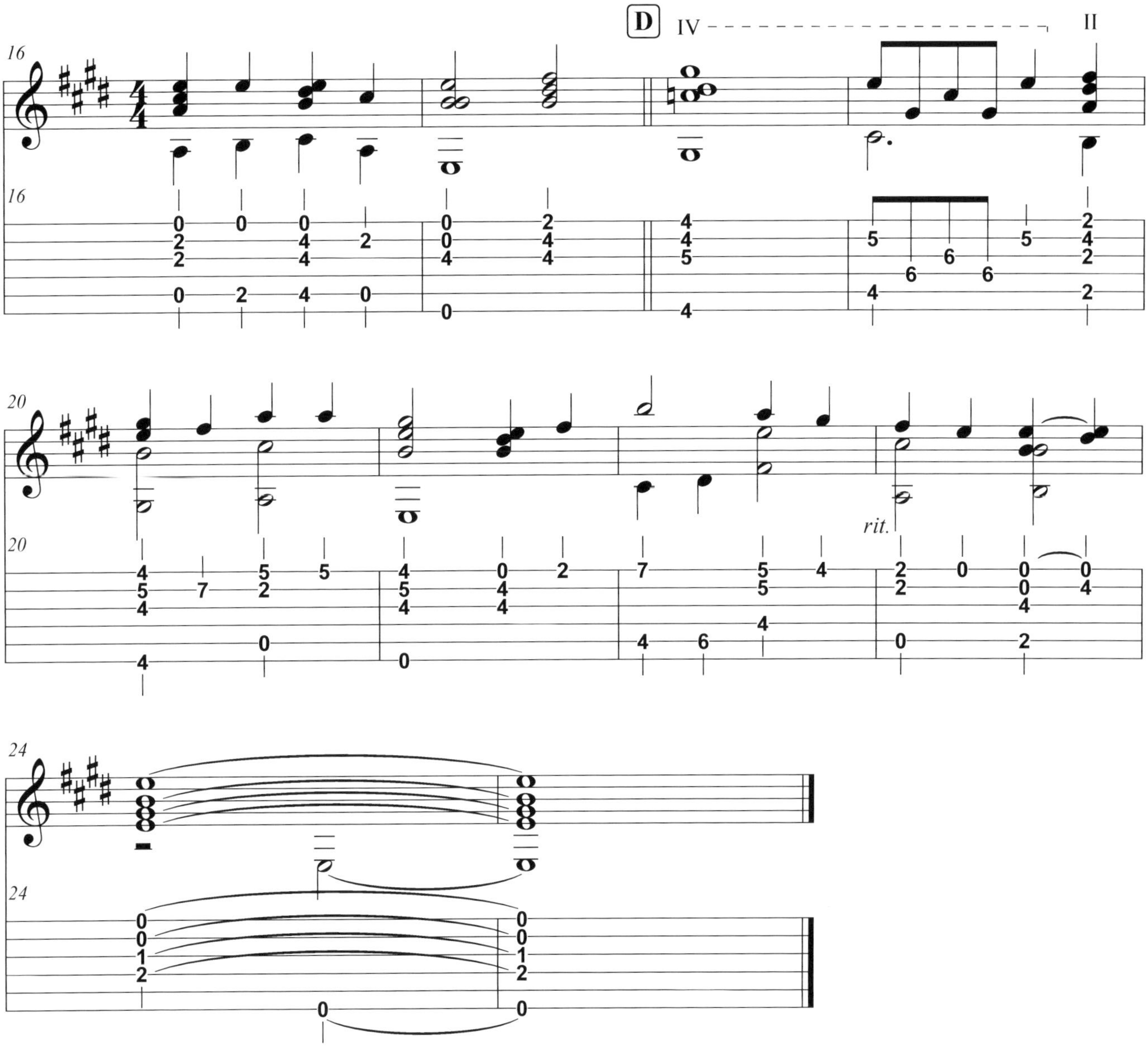
D
IV
II
16
20
rit.
24

On the Cold Ground

John Playford
arr. Raymond Gonzalez

♩. = 50

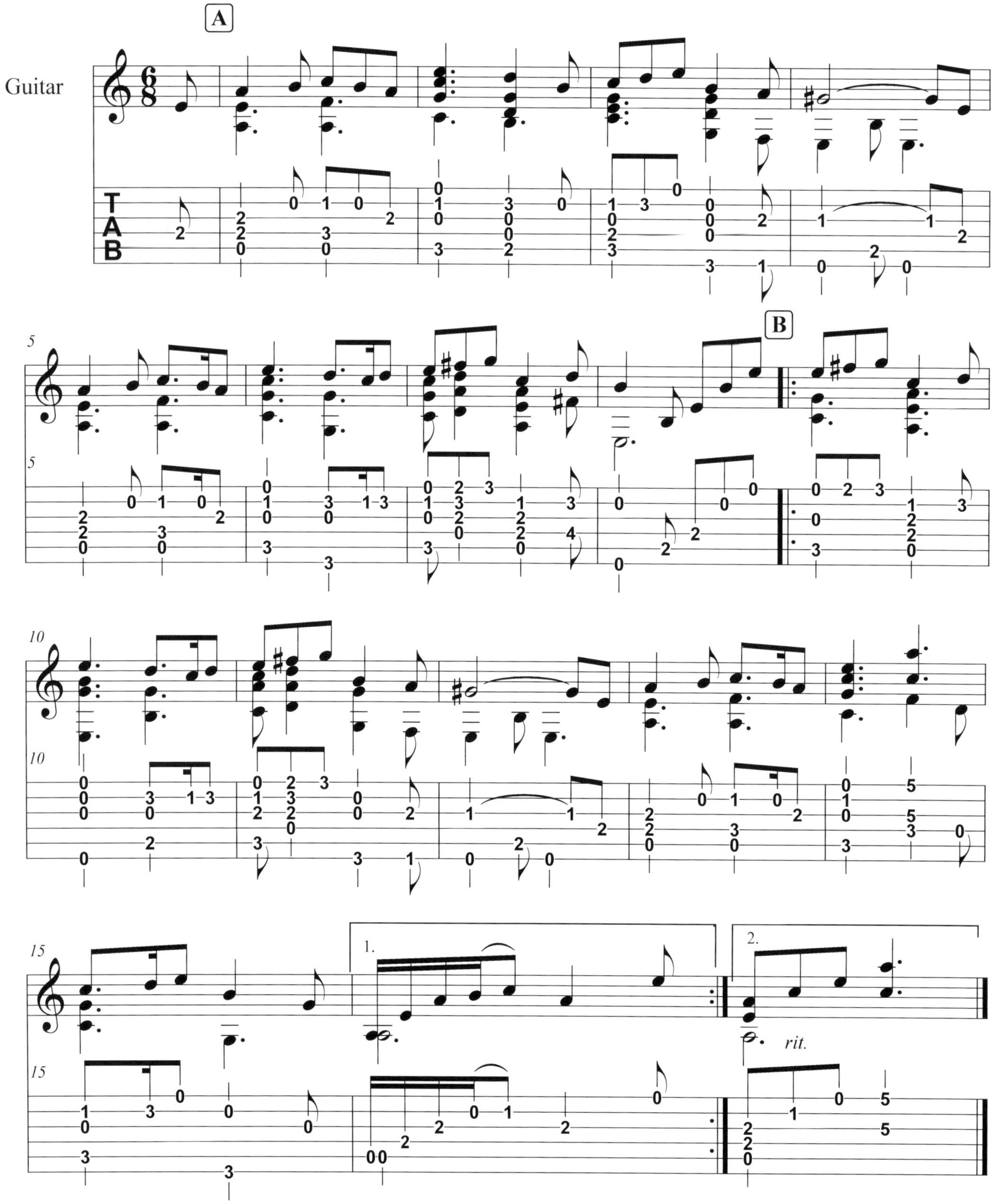

28

Saltarello

⑥ = D

♩ = 100

Vincenzo Galilei
arr. Raymond Gonzalez

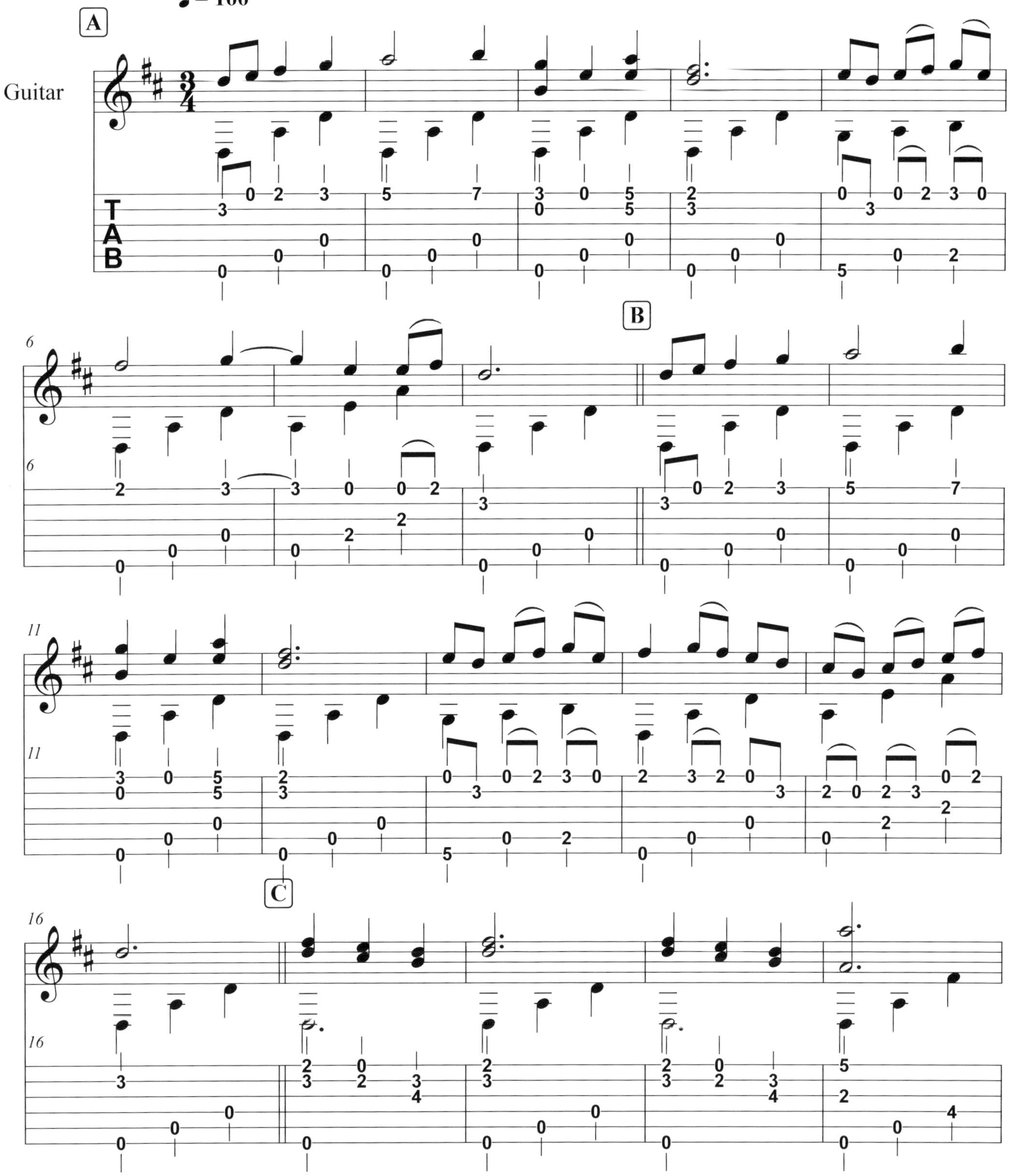

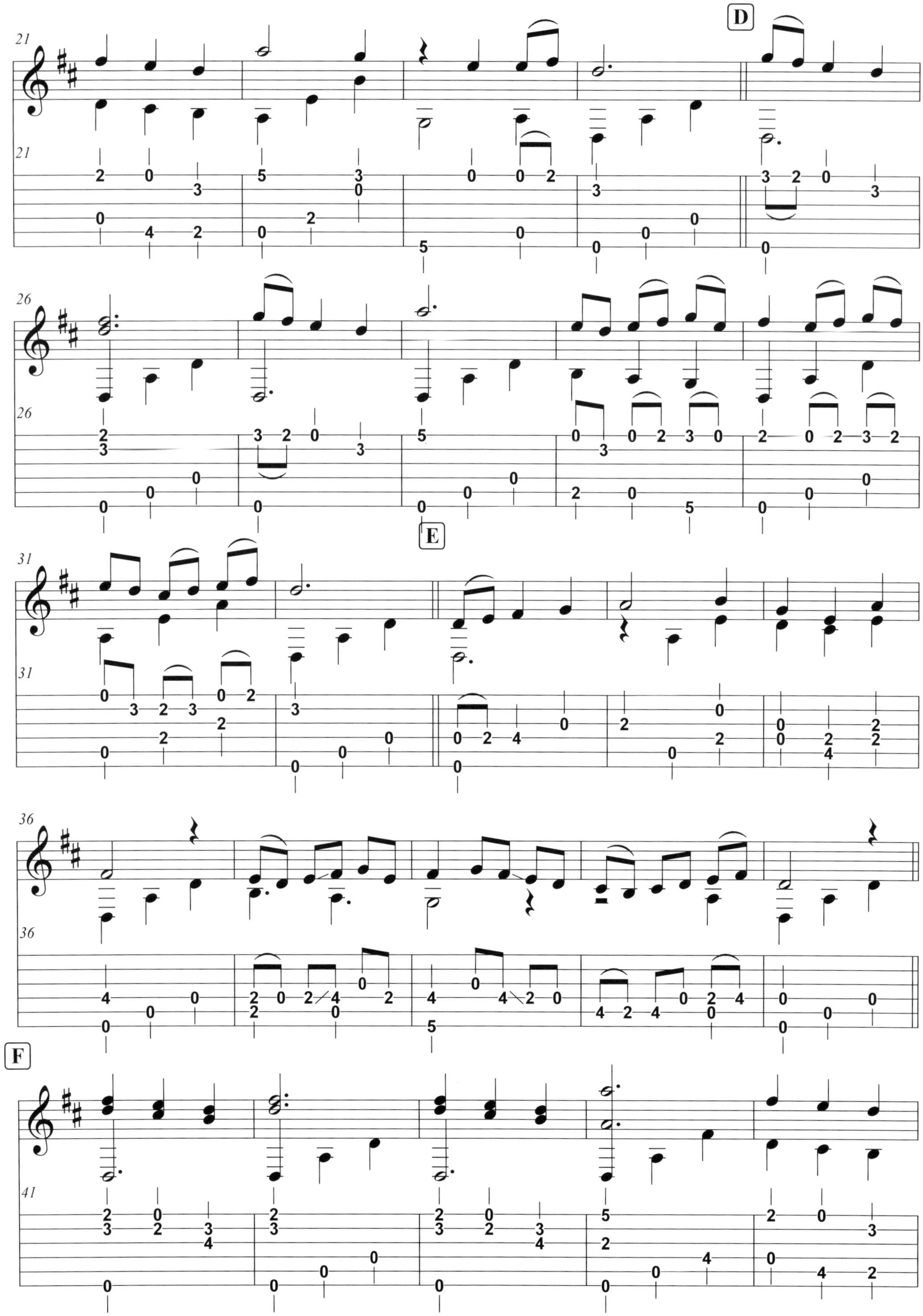
21
D
26
31
E
36
F
41

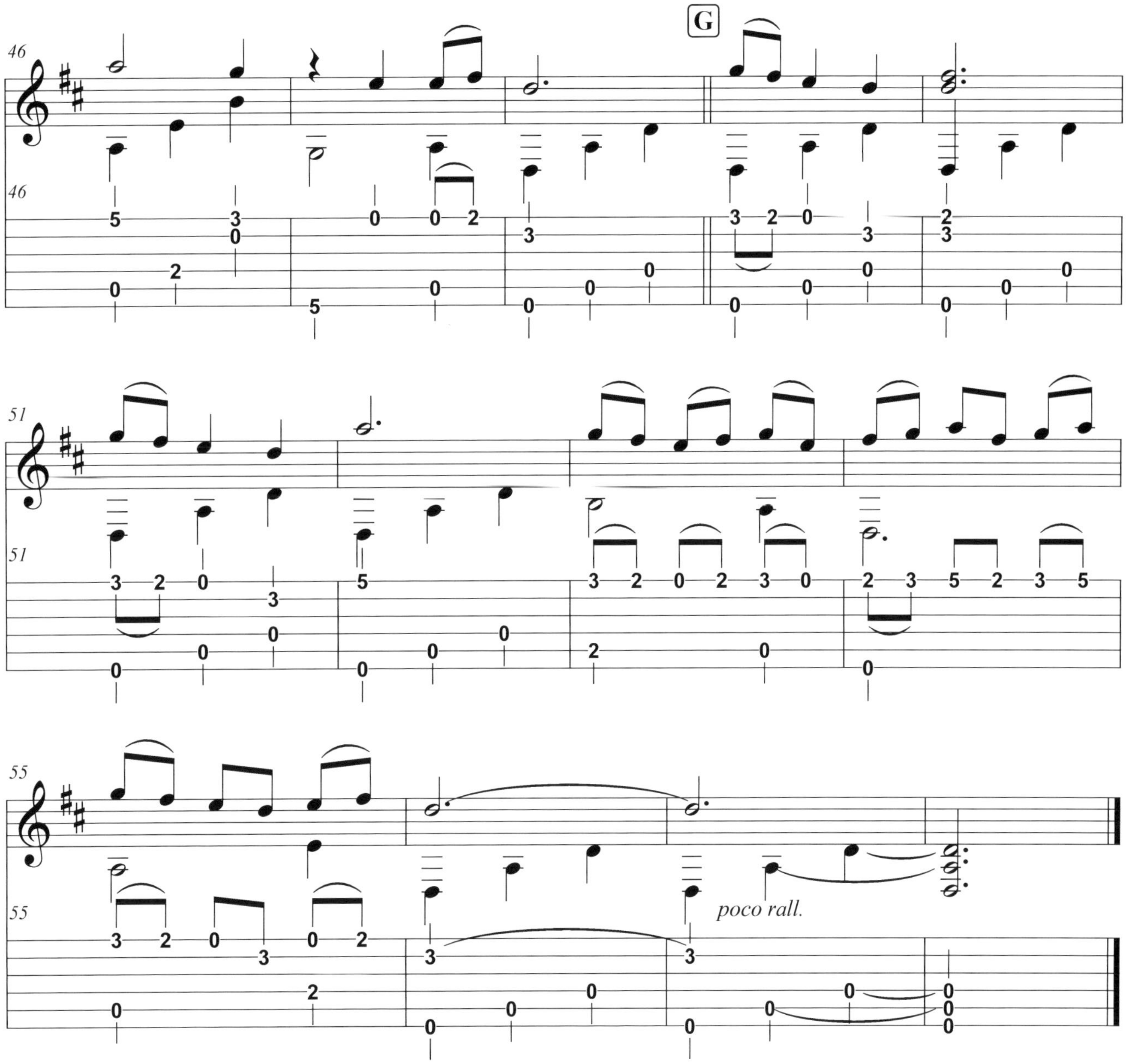
G
poco rall.

29

Si Pour

arr. Raymond Gonzalez

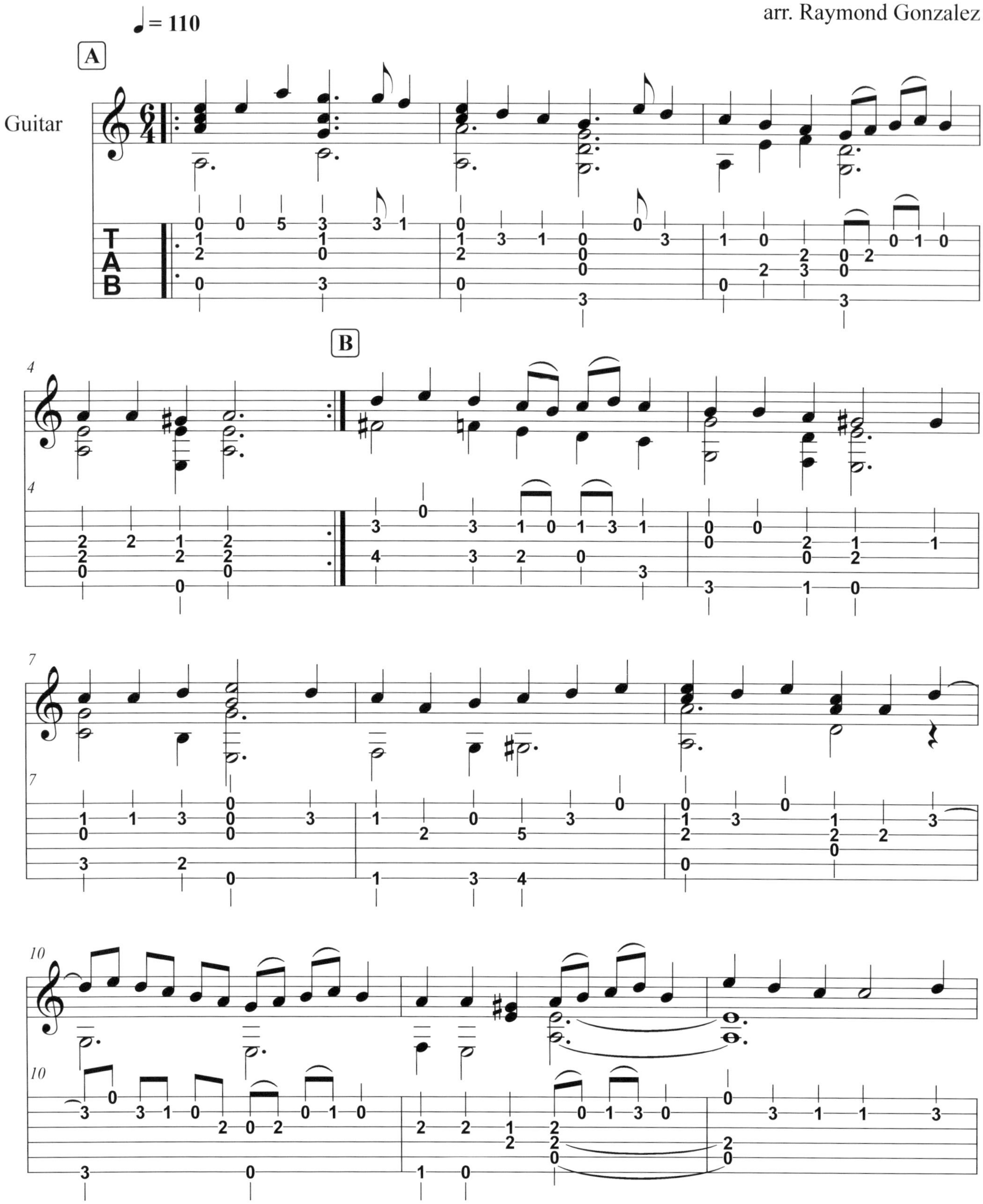

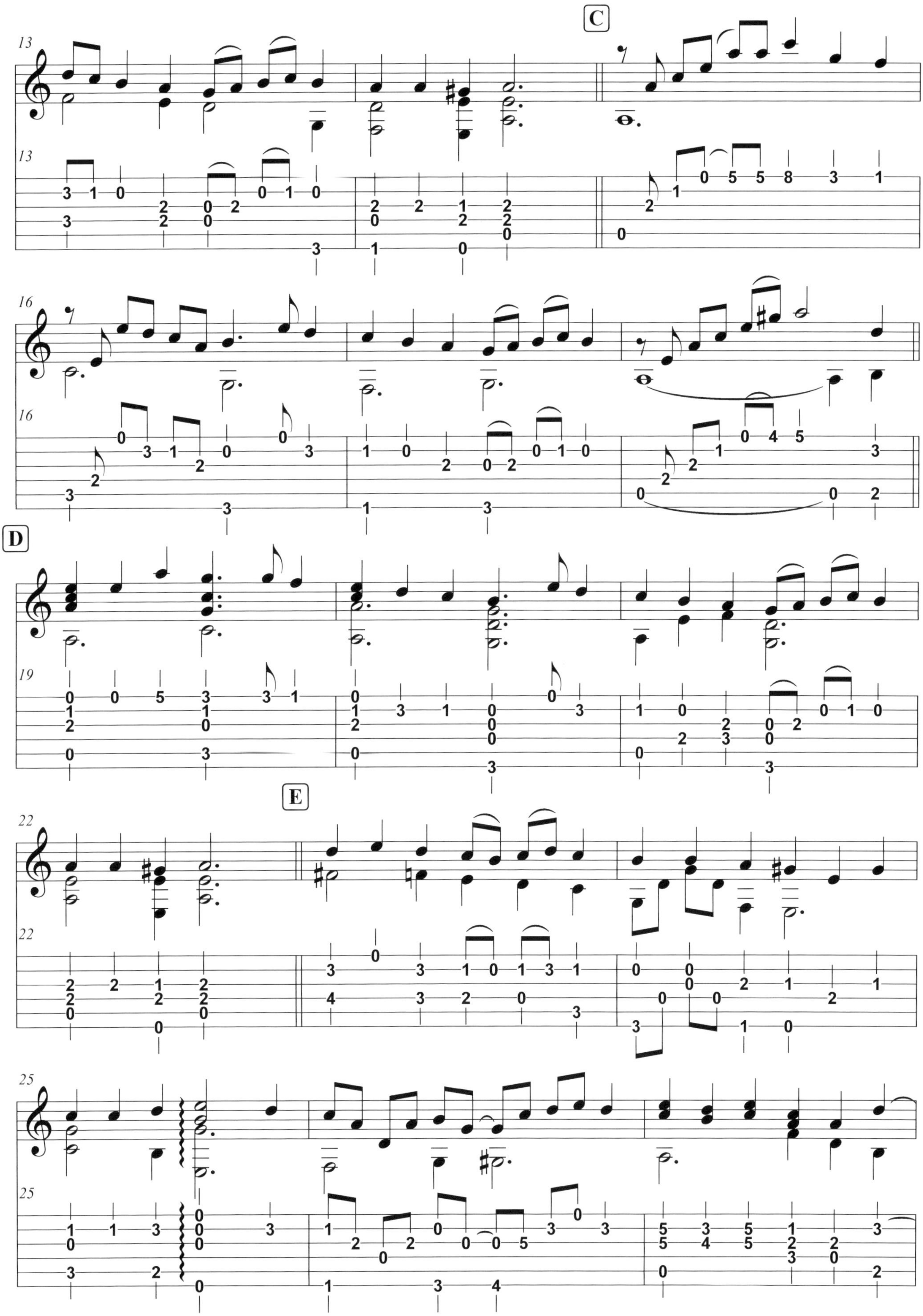
13
C
16
D
19
E
22
25

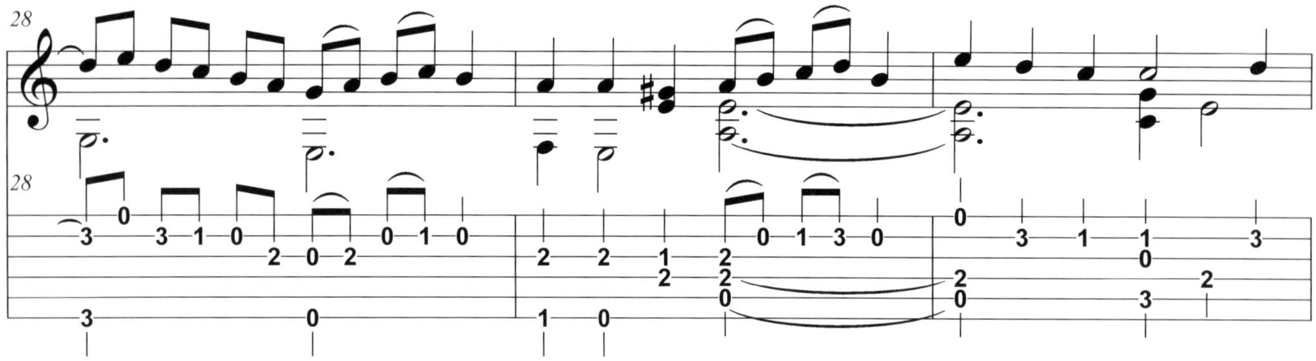

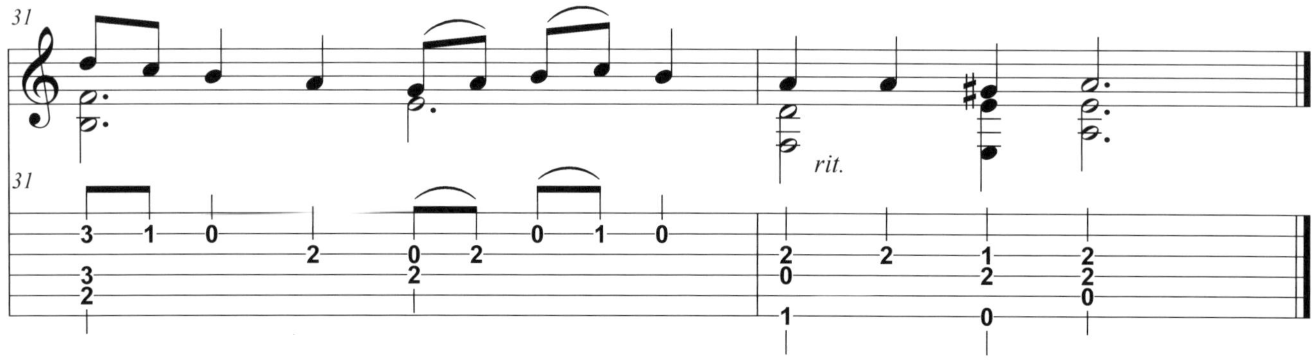
rit.

This page has been left blank to avoid an awward page turn.

30

Spagnoletta

Michael Praetorious
arr. Raymond Gonzalez

♩ = 120

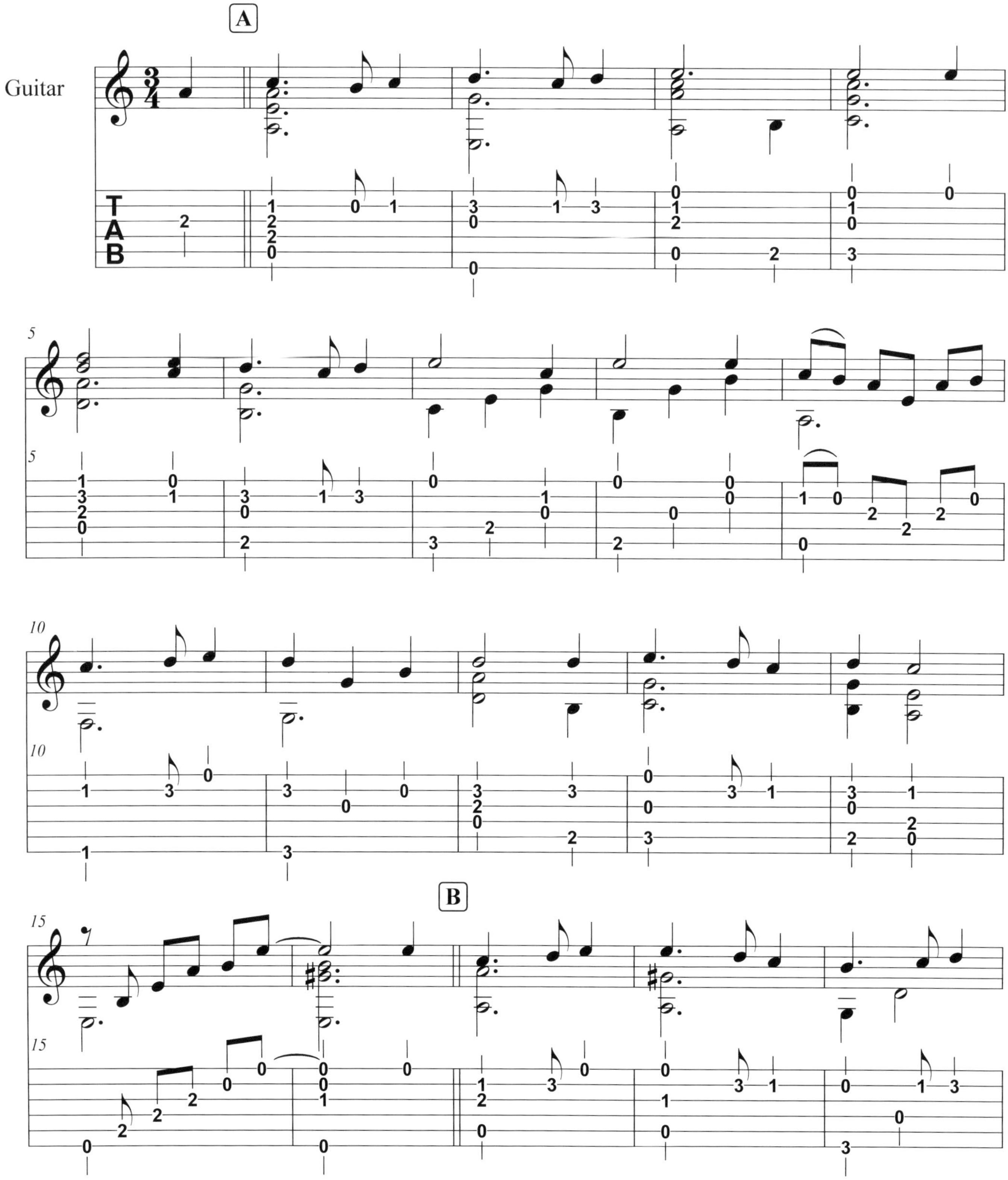

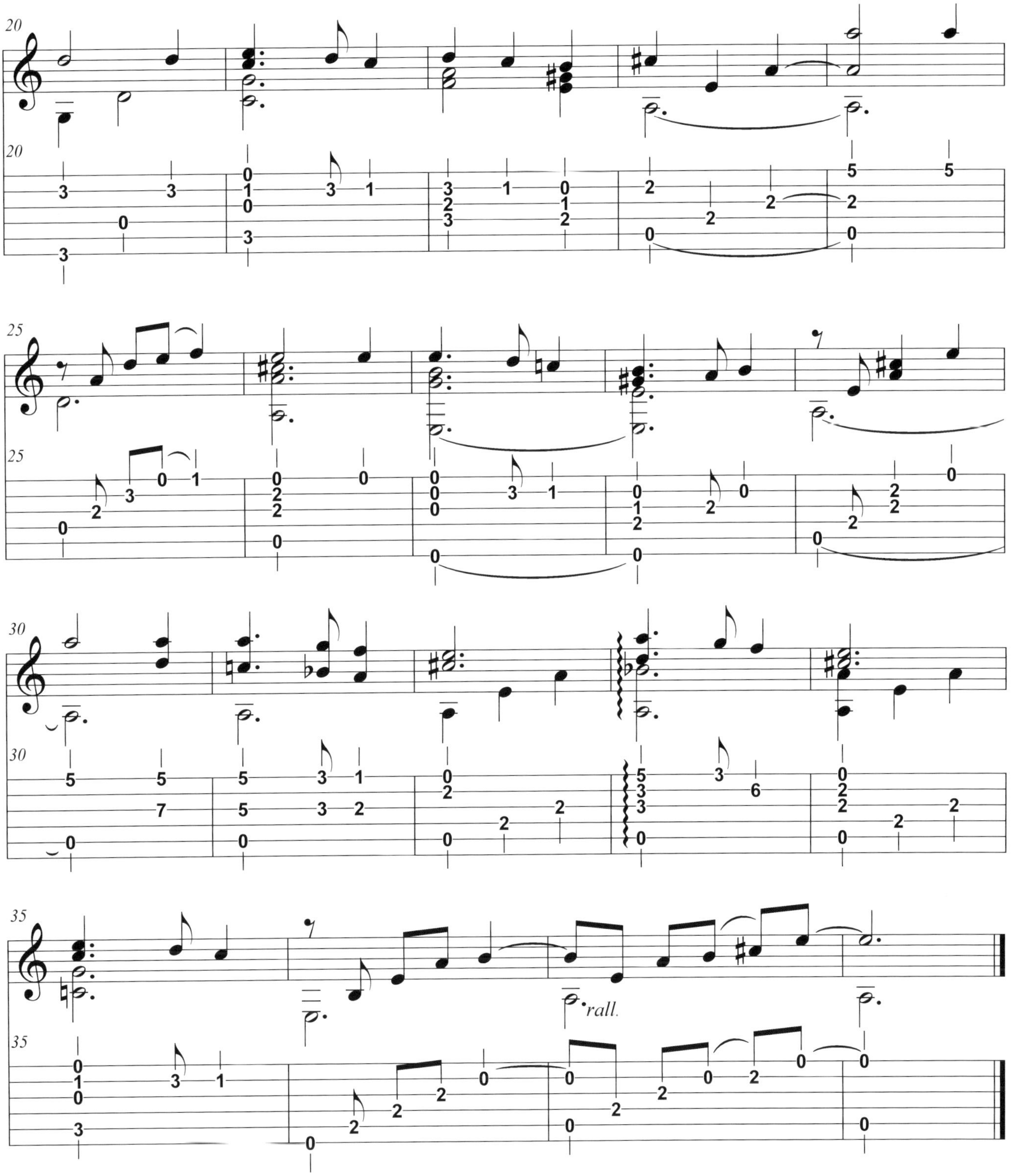
rall.

31

To Drive the Cold Winter Away

Moderate (♪=127)

arr. Raymond Gonzalez

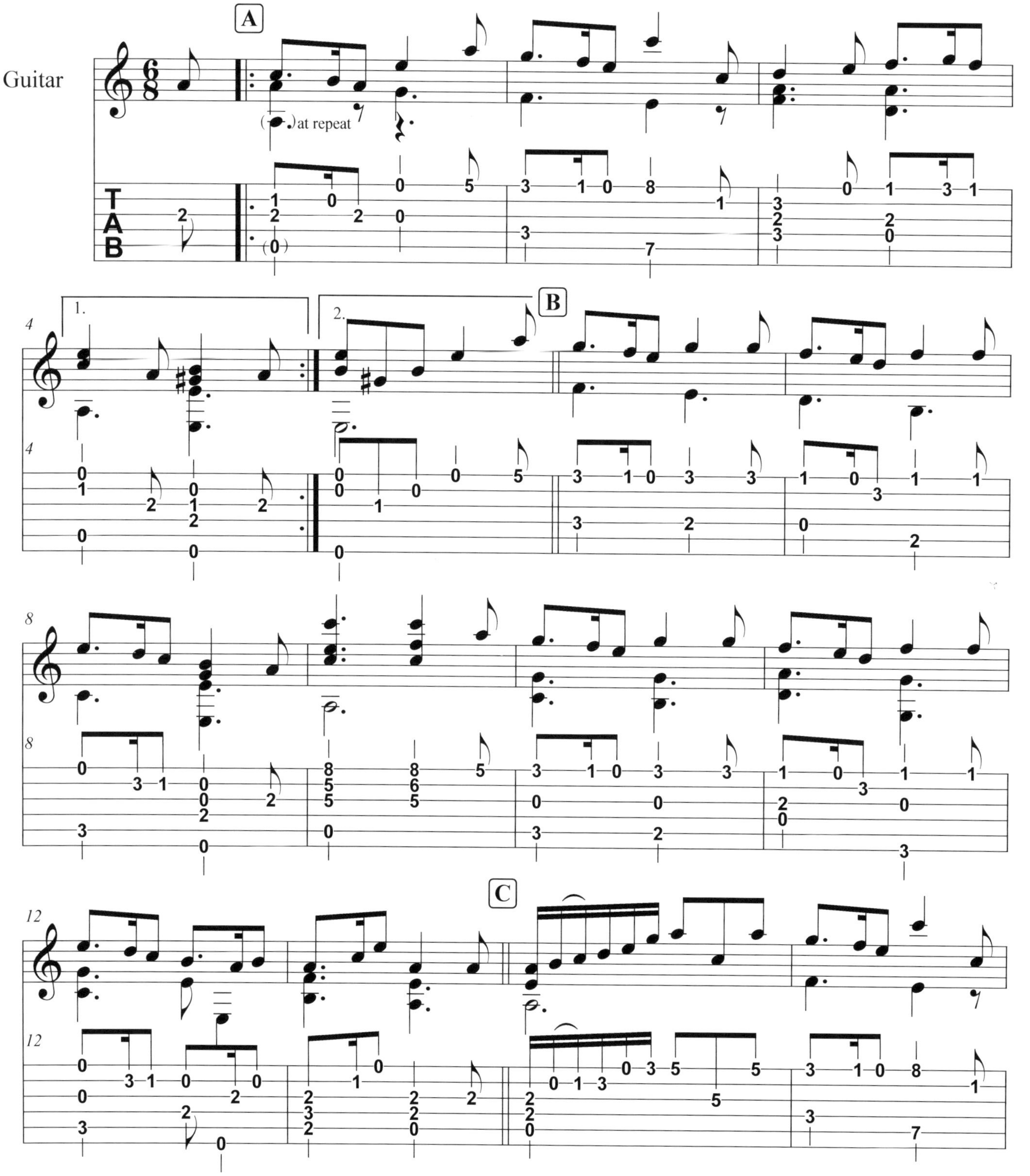

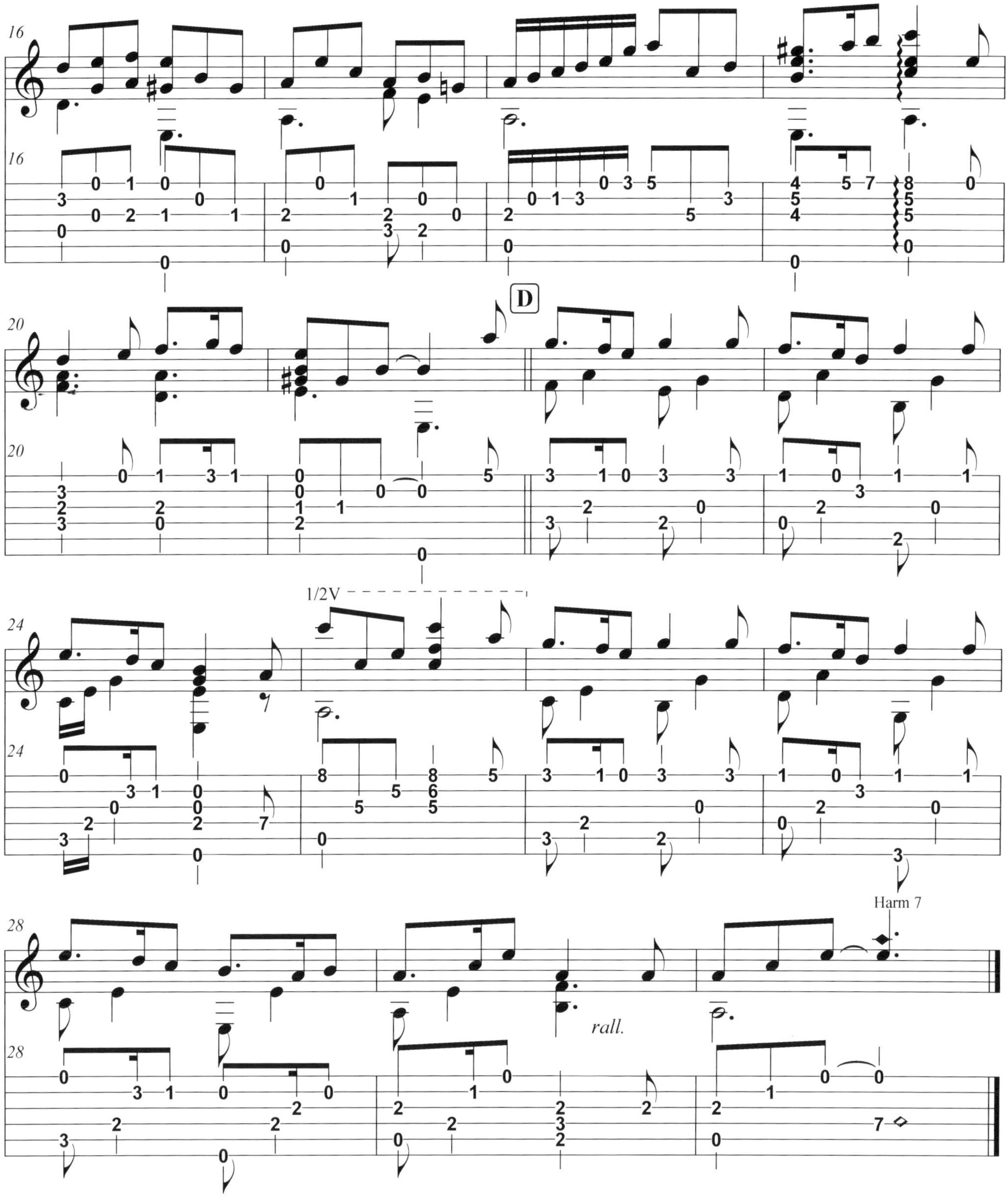
16
D
20
1/2V
24
Harm 7
28
rall.

32

St. Martin's

John Playford
arr. Raymond Gonzalez

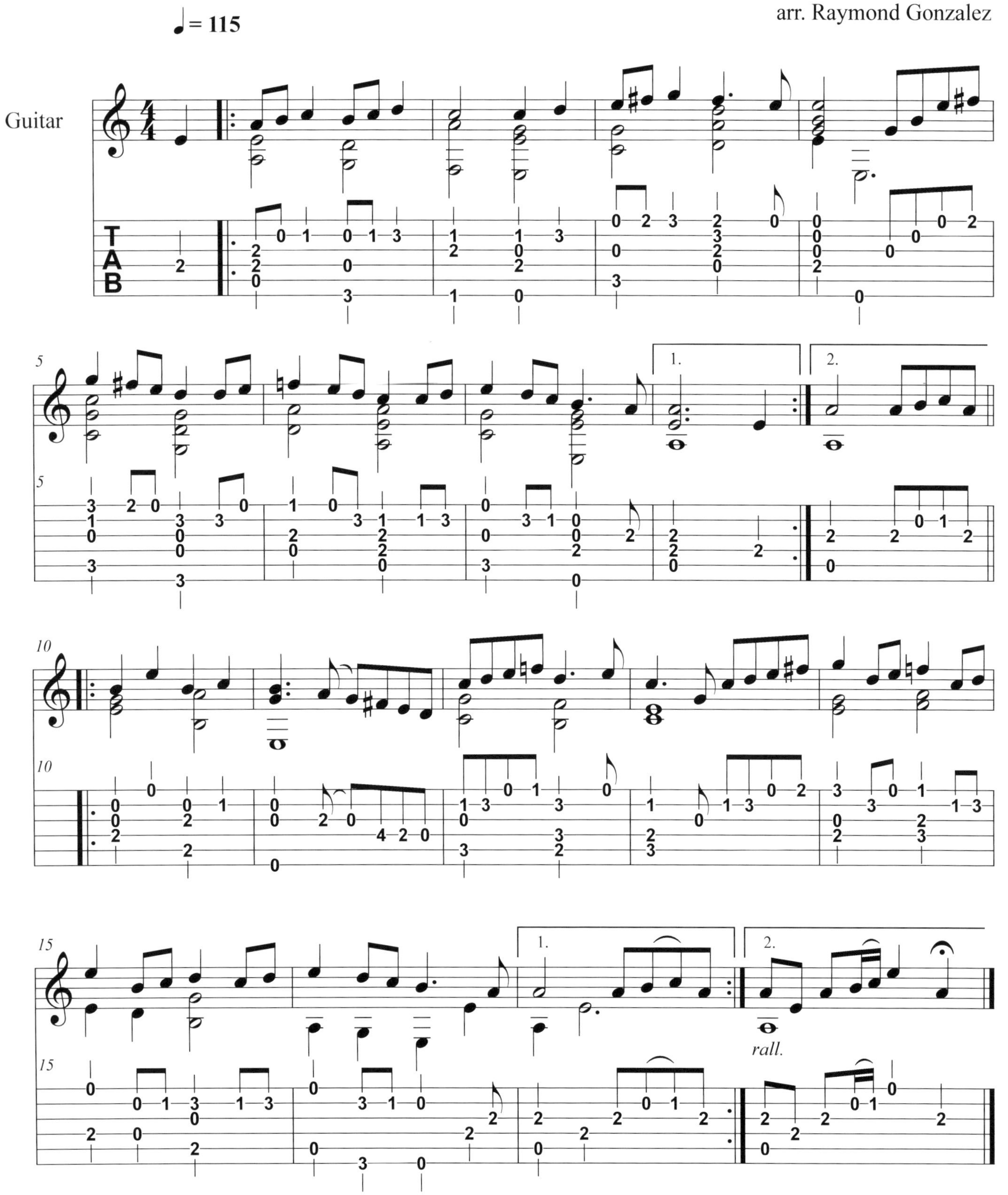

33

Tutte Venite Armati

arr. Raymond Gonzalez

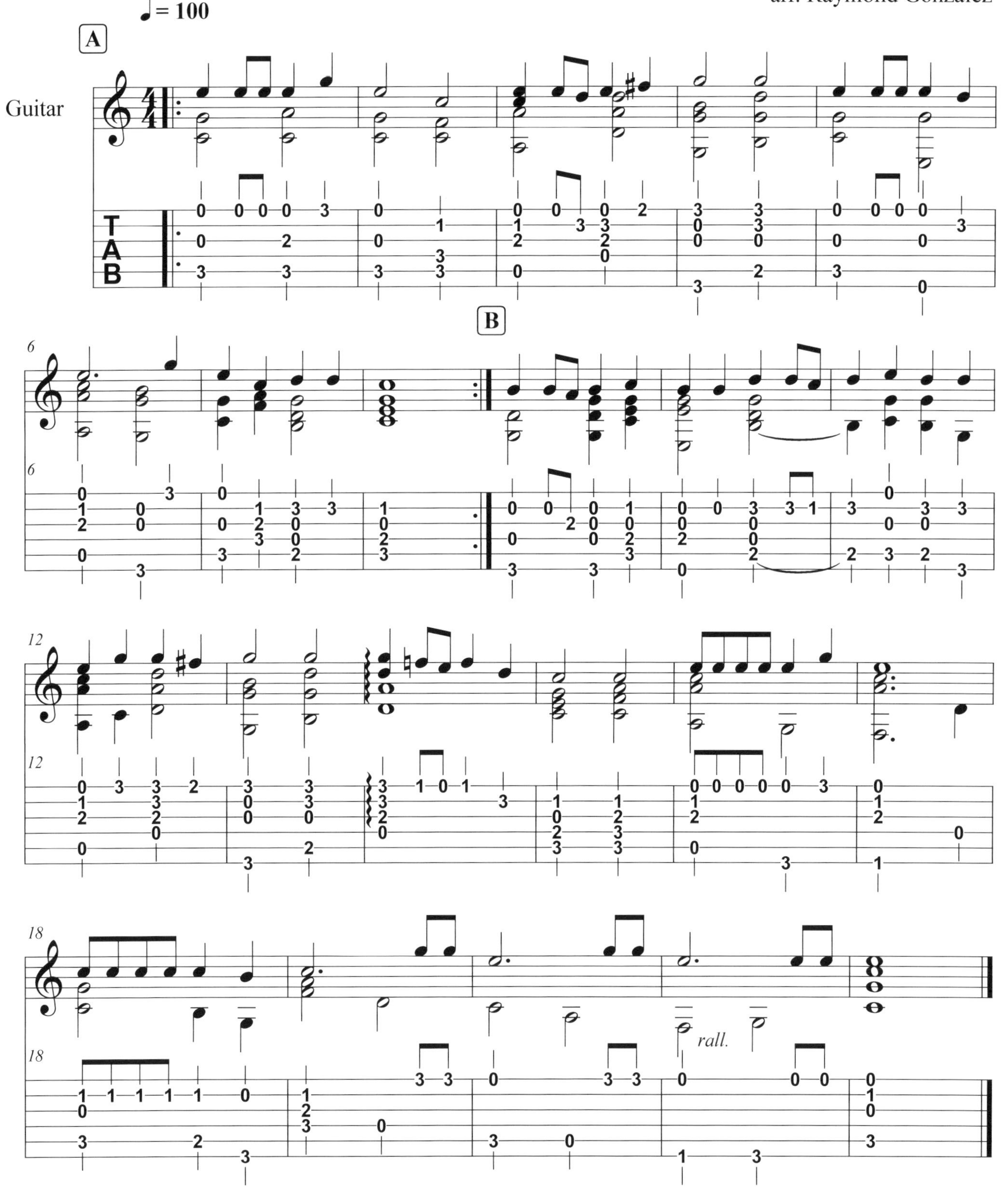

34

Wilson's Wilde

Allegro ♪=145

arr. Raymond Gonzalez

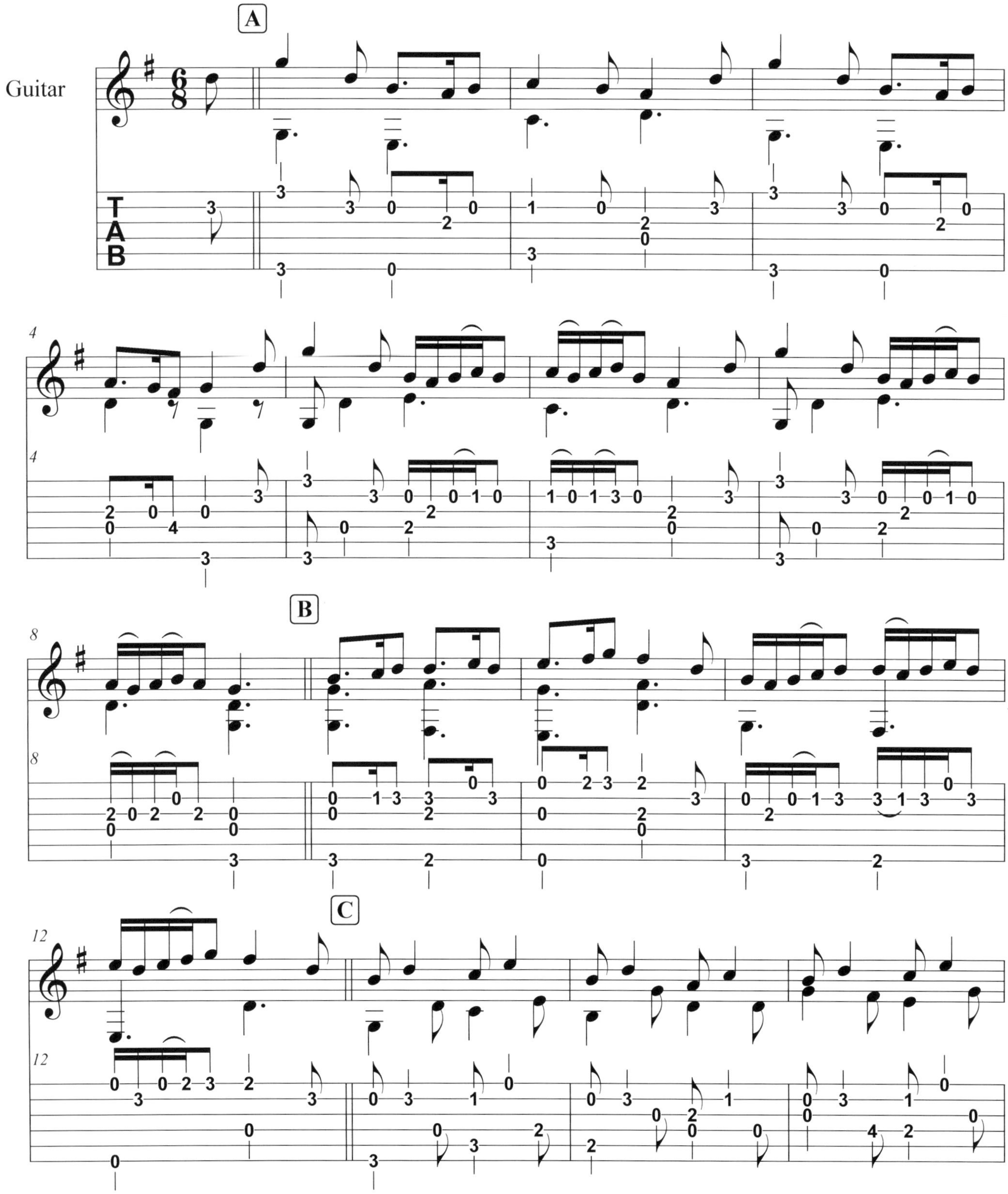

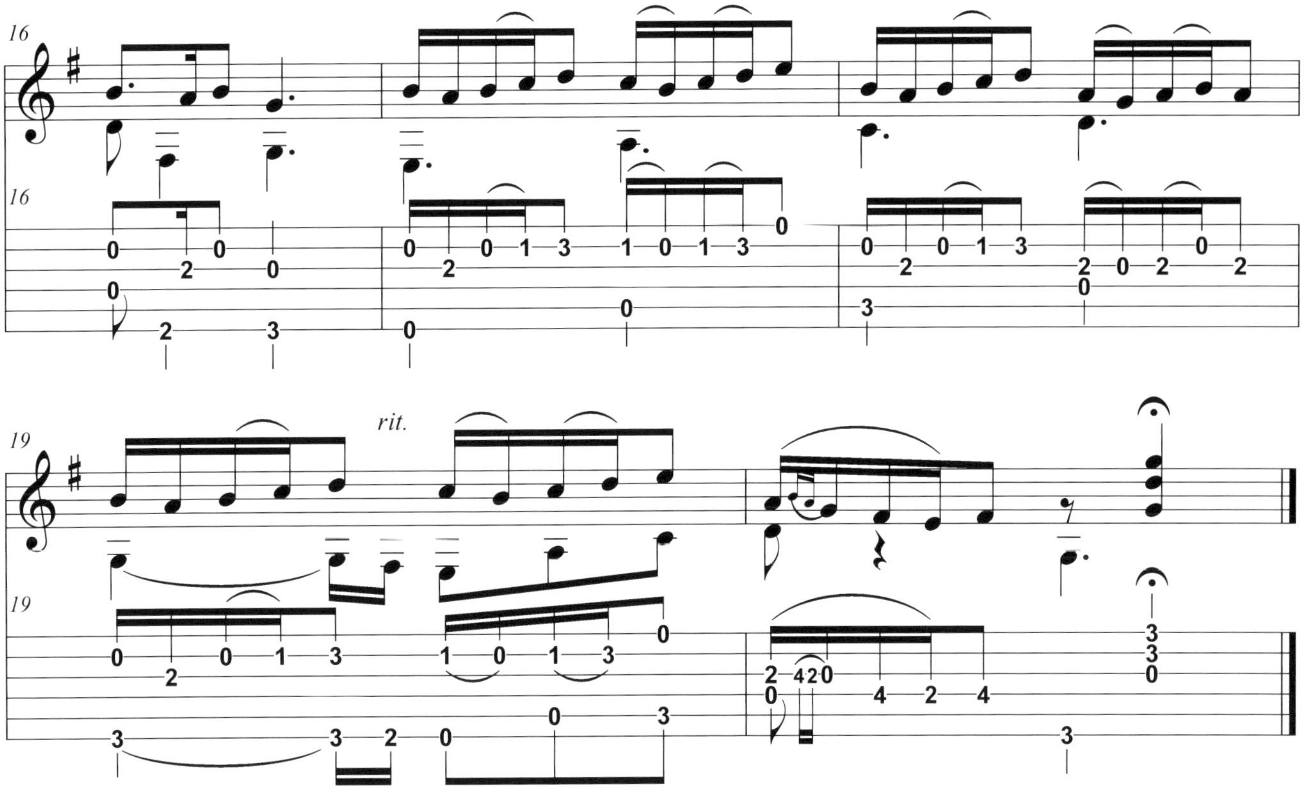
rit.

35

Volte

Michael Praetorius
arr. Raymond Gonzalez

Allegro ♩ = 115

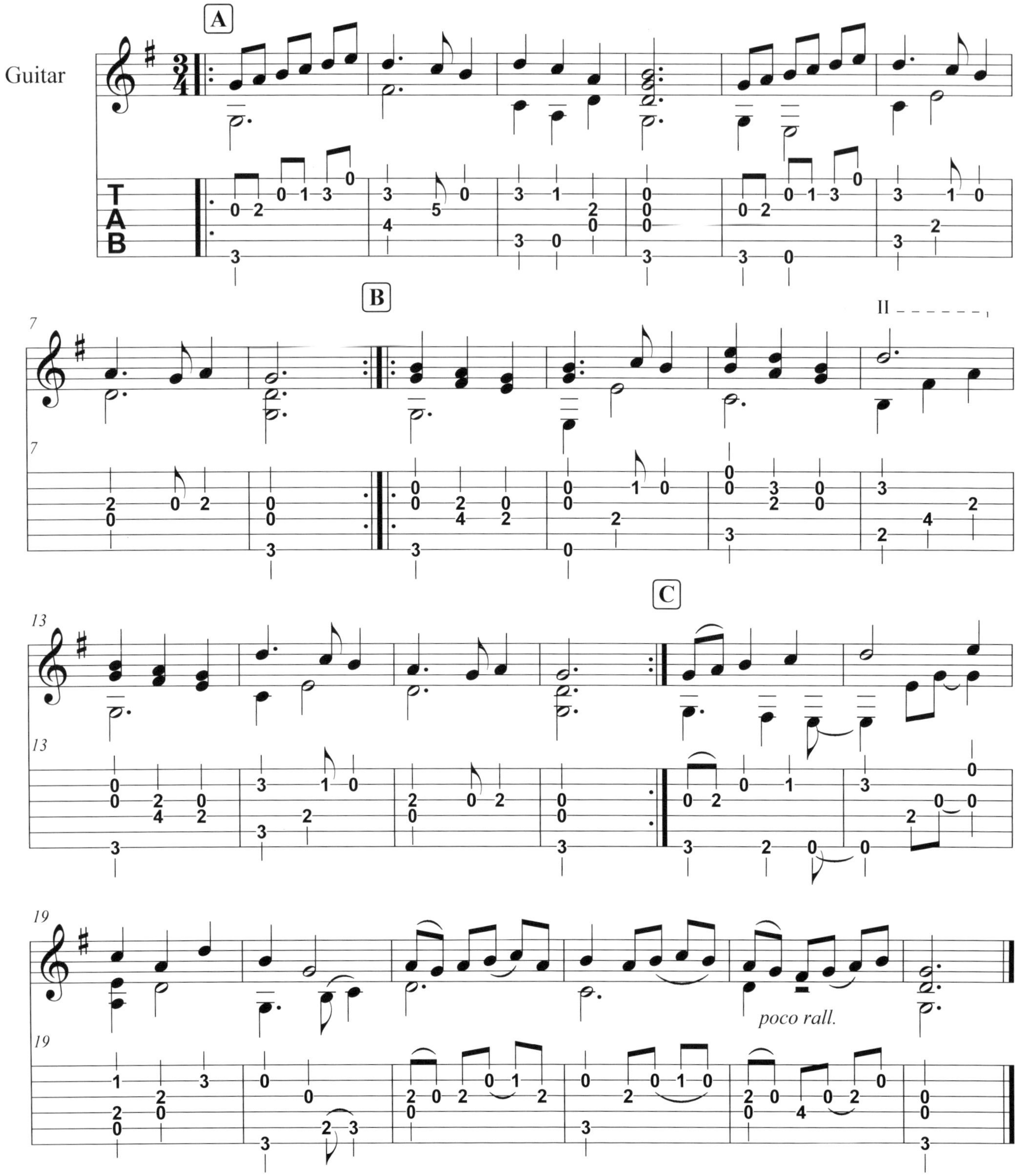